Honoured

Naz Shah has been the Labour MP for Bradford West since her election in 2015 in a bruising battle with George Galloway's Respect Party. She was born in Bradford but sent to Pakistan by her mother at the age of twelve to escape the attentions of her mother's abusive partner. There, she was forced into a marriage at the age of fifteen. When she was twenty, her mother was convicted of the murder of her partner. Naz was instrumental in campaigning and securing her mother's release from prison. *Honoured* is her first book.

Honoured

Survival, Strength and My Path to Politics

NAZ SHAH

First published in Great Britain in 2026 by Weidenfeld & Nicolson,
an imprint of The Orion Publishing Group Ltd
Carmelite House, 50 Victoria Embankment
London EC4Y 0DZ

An Hachette UK Company

The authorised representative in the EEA is Hachette Ireland,
8 Castlecourt Centre, Dublin 15, D15 XTP3, Ireland (email: info@hbgi.ie)

3 5 7 9 10 8 6 4 2

Copyright © Naseem Akhtar Shah 2026

The moral right of Naseem Shah to be identified as
the author of this work has been asserted in accordance
with the Copyright, Designs and Patents Act of 1988.

All rights reserved. No part of this publication may be
reproduced, stored in a retrieval system, or transmitted
in any form or by any means, electronic, mechanical,
photocopying, recording, or otherwise, without the
prior permission of both the copyright owner and the
above publisher of this book.

A CIP catalogue record for this book is
available from the British Library.

ISBN (Hardback) 978 1 3996 2847 1
ISBN (Ebook) 978 1 3996 2849 5
ISBN (Audio) 978 1 3996 2850 1

Typeset by Input Data Services Ltd, Bridgwater, Somerset

Printed in Great Britain by Clays Ltd, Elocgraf, S.p.A.

www.weidenfeldandnicolson.co.uk
www.orionbooks.co.uk

For my mother, my brother and my sister,
with gratitude for the journey thus far.

For my children, Leyana, Aydan and Raese,
with love for all that lies ahead.

Contents

Introduction 1

1. Brown Girl in the Ring 11
2. Legrams Lane 29
3. A Respectable Businessman 43
4. From Bradford to Buffalo 54
5. Nikah 70
6. A Mattress for a Man 76
7. On Remand 86
8. Sofa Surfer 105
9. Bye-Bye Bradford 120
10. Southall Black Sisters 135
11. The Birth of an Activist 145
12. A Broken Woman 158
13. A Suitable Boy 168
14. Freedom, at Last 182
15. Mouse on a Treadmill 191
16. A Meeting Above a Restaurant 201
17. Dreams of My Mother 209
18. Member of Parliament 227

Epilogue 241
Acknowledgements 251

Introduction

The day before the general election of 2015, I received a call from my brother, Imy. The following day, 7 May, the voters of Bradford West would decide who was going to represent them in Parliament as their new MP. Everyone's attention was focused on the head-to-head confrontation between me, the Labour candidate who had been selected to fight the seat just two months earlier, and George Galloway, the incumbent MP who had taken Bradford West from Labour back in 2012 with a majority of 10,140 votes, representing a niche, very left-wing party called Respect. Could I take back Bradford West for the Party?

My brother got straight to the point.

'Right,' he said. 'We're having a meeting.'

'A meeting? What meeting?' I was too busy for this.

'You, me and Foz,' he went on. 'We're having a meeting today, Naz.'

'Are you joking?' I asked. 'It's the flipping election tomorrow, Imy; I'm in *meetings* all day, every day. Every hour. And you want me to come and hang out with you and Foz?' Fozia is our sister.

'That's right,' he said calmly.

Imy can be stubborn at times, but this exchange was

especially irksome given that I was about to face one of the greatest challenges of my life.

'I want you round at mine tonight at nine o'clock. We'll be waiting for you.'

At that time, Imy lived in a house on Ennerdale Road in Bradford, a stone's throw from our sister.

I tried once more to explain just how many people I still had to see, to speak to, to try to win over before the voting booths opened in the morning, but he was implacable.

'I know you've got meetings, *Baj*' – Baj means big sister, but at that moment, Imy was behaving like the elder sibling – 'but this will be the most important meeting of your election. Nine o'clock,' he repeated. 'Sharp.'

I sighed. 'All right. Nine o'clock.'

It had been a hard campaign. Little did I know then that I'd face even nastier attacks in the next election, but the battle with George Galloway had been intense. Among some British Pakistani families, there exists a form of almost invisible networking known as *baradari* – a deeply patriarchal clan system rooted in the established hierarchies of northeast Pakistan. When young men began arriving in Bradford in the 1950s to work in the mills and factories, they built a close-knit community and relied on each other for support. Over time, their dreams of returning to Pakistan faded. There were jobs in Britain and superior educational opportunities for their children. When people started to turn to the better educated among them for guidance, these men began to represent the migrant families in local politics and gradually became established community leaders. As their influence grew, it became clear that no political party could

INTRODUCTION

succeed in Bradford without the backing of these baradari leaders.

Of course, informal networks like this aren't new – they exist in every culture. Old Etonians spring to mind. In Bradford, the influence of the baradari system, and the men who dominate it, remains strong to this day.

There had certainly been some clear attempts to derail my campaign by patriarchal community leaders, who would have preferred to see Galloway reinstated rather than watch a mouthy woman, with her vocal support for women's rights and women's equality, win the seat. The baradari, with one eye always on the line of succession, were keen to hold on to power and control Bradford policy.

The fusing of clan allegiances with politics is a dangerous one that creates gatekeepers to essential services. Ordinarily, one would call the council if there were issues with bin collections or potholes on local roads. But many from the Pakistani community are often not aware of the correct channels. Language can be an issue, too, so instead they call clan leaders, effectively empowering them as the ones who can give access to the things people need, such as everyday services. In turn, these clan leaders hold on to their power by deliberately bypassing or obstructing proper channels for reform.

Given that I wasn't part of any baradari family, and I was a women's rights activist who wouldn't be controlled by these men, I had my work cut out for me. In 2012, George Galloway won his seat by avoiding the baradari and appealing directly to women, but in 2015 he jumped onto the baradari bandwagon, recognising they would never support me and instead harnessed their power for his own gain.

INTRODUCTION

Early on in the campaign, I'd written in a blog post published on International Women's Day why I was so passionate about the rights of women everywhere. I explained how my mother had been handed a life sentence in 1993 for murdering the man who had abused her for years, and how, in the years leading up to the murder, she had been abandoned by her husband and family, left in the grip of poverty and forced to move from inadequate accommodation to inadequate accommodation with three young children in tow, in an attempt to find us a secure and safe home. I outlined how, after Mum's sentence and incarceration, me and my younger siblings had learnt how to survive on our own, clinging to each other. I had become the head of my family at just eighteen, and we continued our peripatetic lives. I explained to potential voters how we'd kept ourselves going, how we'd fought for Mum's release and how I'd begun to campaign on behalf of women in Bradford facing discrimination due to disability.

I focused on disability advocacy because, throughout my childhood, Mum had been a carer for disabled children, and I was comfortable working in this area. Disabled people don't receive the same access to services and support as the able-bodied; they receive even less access if they're brown and less still if they're brown women.

We were a working-class family. I left school at twelve when Mum sent me to Pakistan to escape the attentions of her abusive partner. I spent my early teenage years in a remote village cleaning up buffalo shit – in retrospect, maybe not a bad training for British politics. In 2015, I wasn't just fighting to win the seat of Bradford West; I was fighting for everyone

INTRODUCTION

I'd ever met who had suffered from discrimination based on class, sex or colour.

While we'd waited for Mum to be released (and we'd wait fourteen long years), the three of us had made lives for ourselves. We married, had children and forged ahead in our chosen careers. We mastered resilience and I was as proud of Imy and Foz's achievements as I was of my own. They were part of my journey, part of my campaign to offer myself up to the people of Bradford West to stand as their representative in Parliament in the general election. So, yes, of course I was going to drop everything and heed the call of my siblings to attend a 'meeting' at Imy's at nine o'clock.

When I arrived, my sister-in-law, Imy's wife, ushered me into the front room.

'They're waiting for you,' she told me.

Imy and Foz were sitting on the floor by the bay window. The room was bathed in candlelight.

'Right, Baj,' Imy said. 'Go and do your *wudu* and then come and sit with us.'

Once I'd performed my pre-prayer ritual ablutions I joined my siblings. Imy began to read from the Qur'an and then the three of us quietly began to perform *dhikr*, the spiritual practice we Muslims call the Remembrance of God.

'Allāhu, Allāhu, Allāhu,' we chanted.

Dhikr feels very like meditation and while the three of us sat still on the floor, chanting the word over and over, it wasn't long before we were all in tears. We were crying for the long, often tortured journey we had taken together. We cried because we knew how far we'd come, and for every challenge

INTRODUCTION

we had overcome, every slight we had endured. And we cried with joy because we were together right now, whole and happy. Mum wasn't with us, she was looking after my kids, but she was there in spirit and in love and in the knowledge of the path we had all taken.

The next day, while the voters were still streaming in and out of the election booths, I saw George Galloway riding the same election bus he'd used in his original 2012 campaign. Back then, his bus was crammed with supporters. This time, he had just one other person with him – his wife. He didn't look like a winner this time around and I knew victory was mine.

When the results finally came in, we'd overturned Galloway's previous majority of 10,000 votes and won a majority for Labour of 11,420.

I was honoured by the people of Bradford West to be their MP.

I still am.

I had been thinking about writing this book for a long time. Friends had suggested I tell my story for years.

In April 2023, I was able to enjoy one of the great privileges of my life: along with my three children, I made the journey to Mecca for *Umrah*, the Muslim pilgrimage to our holiest place on earth. I can't tell you how proud I was of my kids – to see them so strong and beautiful and faithful, performing their rites in the holy city. And as can often happen when a believer visits Mecca for Umrah or *Hajj*, I found myself deeply moved by the spirituality of the occasion. As I circled the Ka'aba – the granite building in the centre of our most

INTRODUCTION

holy site – in the time-prescribed way, I felt an overwhelming sense of both peace and anticipation, and a proud gratitude that I had achieved so much for my family and in my career, as well as a strong intuition that I still have work to do.

I have been a highly visible figure to many over the years, and that has brought both benefits and penalties. I have made profound and lasting connections with an amazing number of individuals in the UK and around the world. I've also been attacked and denigrated – possibly more than most British MPs – often for the 'sin' of being a vocal, feminist, Asian Muslim woman. One evening, as I sat watching the sunset in Mecca, I had a thought that wouldn't go away: it was time to reclaim my story.

Having shifted the dial over the last eight years towards greater prosperity in Bradford, I am not complacent. I know I still have work to do. I have no wish for my time as an MP to come to an end only to watch corrupting influences – such as the powerful local families – return to their former strength.

I want to see Bradford take its rightful place alongside other successful northern cities such as Leeds and Manchester. I want education levels to keep improving and investment to keep coming in. I want pockets of poverty raised out of where they currently lie. I don't see any poverty of aspiration or ability in my constituency of Bradford West, but I do still see a lack of infrastructure to support the people who want to grow. That's what we have to keep working towards.

As a global Muslim ambassador, I also want to promote the health and safety of my faith community – a community that makes up one quarter of the world's population. I want to keep combatting the scourge of Islamophobia and racism

INTRODUCTION

wherever they appear. I want to work for peace in troubled areas, whether in Kashmir or Palestine, so that people of all communities can be allowed to live as they should live: in peace and freedom.

As a Muslim, I see it as my responsibility every day to bring out the best in people. To have faith in humanity. This is a responsibility that goes beyond faith; it's a desire to see every single person, no matter what they believe, given the opportunity to fulfil their potential. Does that sounds idealistic? Then tell me a better vision.

As I watched the sunset in Mecca, I made a decision. To reclaim my narrative, I would set out the events of my life – events that brought me to where I stand today. By telling my story, I hope to show others why I feel this sense of anticipation and why I believe there is still so much more good to come.

This is a story about me, my mum and my family. I worried about how much I should reveal of Mum's life and I've sought advice from spiritual advisors, family members and friends. There is a strong tradition within Islam – a religion deeply rooted in notions of peace and calm and respect – that painful events should be left alone, in the past. Let sleeping dogs lie. Don't rake over the ashes. Don't rock the boat. And yet, there is also a powerful spiritual command to be truthful always, to allow the heart to be open; that however bitter the truth might be, it is better out than in – particularly if the events of the past led to a positive future.

What happened to my family revolved around the notion of *honour*. A simple word to most, but within my culture, it's

INTRODUCTION

a loaded term. It's a tree with deep roots, spreading far and wide, dictating every aspect of how we live.

If Mum were to protect the honour of our family, she would have to remain silent about the terrible years of her abuse. If it wasn't for the honour, or *izzat*, of the community, Mum might have been able to ask for help when she was coerced into a brutal and abusive 'relationship'. If the community hadn't believed she had lost all her honour, they might have given her support and protection. Honour – that noble term – denied my mother the justice she deserved.

Despite all we've been through, this book isn't what the publishing industry used to call a 'misery memoir'. I consider my story a joyful, optimistic attempt to show how good can come from ill – how we can all take heart in the strength we willingly lend to those around us. Like many others, I hold a deep conviction that we can turn away from the divisions and hostility that characterise today's political arena and build a better world based on trust and mutual support.

I think the times we find ourselves in now are troubling and I know from talking to my constituents that many feel the same way. It may take ten, fifteen, even twenty years to rebuild a society where people feel safe and supported – but that is the objective that I and others are committed to achieving.

But to reach a destination, we each have to reflect upon our own journey. I can't brush aside painful truths or distressing episodes in my life just because they're difficult to hear – or harder still to tell.

There's one person who could stop me in my tracks if she chose to, and that's Mum. But as someone who has spent years clawing back her dignity and honour, she – more than

INTRODUCTION

anyone else – wants me to tell the truth. And it is only by laying everything bare that we can find our way home.

The vast majority of us want to live alongside our families and our neighbours in a place we call home and in a spirit of mutual support. That's what I think of when I think of Bradford and I hope it's what you think of, too, when you consider your own town, your own life. Fairness, justice and equality for all are the prizes that await us down this road, and I look forward to the time when we can all share in them together.

So while this book is about me, it's as much about the place that made me – Bradford. I hope, too, that you will reflect on the events in your own life that have helped define who you are and where you call home. Those events aren't always good; sometimes they are incredibly painful. My own story, as you'll discover, is in many ways still raw with suffering. But it has, I am convinced, helped me become the person I believe I should be. The person I am meant to be.

I

Brown Girl in the Ring

Brown girl in the ring, tra la la la la . . .

That's my dad singing. It's 1978 and he's lifting me onto the brown Panasonic TV in the front room of our house. Now he's twirling me around, laughing and singing the Boney M. song, and I'm laughing too and clapping my hands in time to the tune. I'm not even five years old, but I'm the apple of my dad's eye. He loves this song – and he loves me.

Brown girl in the ring.

So charismatic was my dad. Always the best-dressed man on the street, a twinkle in his handsome dark eyes and a ready bag of sweets. The other kids in the neighbourhood loved coming round to our house – we were the only ones with a colour TV. My dad had left his job working the night shift at the mills and set up his own business producing sofas and sofa beds. He had his own factory, employing plenty of men to keep up with the growing demand. I remember the factory – huge piles of foam everywhere. I'd clamber to the top and bounce from one pile to another, treating the whole place like my personal playground. And Dad's employees? They spoilt me rotten, treating me like a little princess.

Dad was six years old when he came to Bradford with his parents from Mirpur in northeast Pakistan. He'd gone to school in Bradford, so for him it was home. Pakistanis from that region of the country began to move to the UK – and to cities like Bradford – in the 1950s, drawn by the promise of full-time employment in the mills and factories of the north of England. The UK was rebuilding after the trauma of war, and the country needed more and more workers to help grow the economy.

Dad had a swagger about him, like he owned whatever place he found himself in. Not my mum, though. She was seventeen when she left Pakistan to come to the UK as Dad's bride; she'd grown up in the countryside and couldn't speak, read or write English. Mum was a homemaker and she followed all the rules.

Brown girl in the ring . . .

Now I'm racing up the steps at the back of our house to get to street level. The Anvil Court back-to-back houses had gardens that sat at the bottom of what felt like very steep stone steps for a five-year-old, but I know I've got to reach the top and find help. Dad is beating my mum and I need another adult to come and stop him. I can hear him shouting as he strikes out. I felt the thump of his fist into her body rippling through my own.

Why was he beating my mum? You might as well ask: why do men all over the world attack women? While Mum was a timid person, she couldn't stand bad language. Maybe she'd told him to stop swearing so much, or maybe she'd burnt the milk for his coffee or just looked at him the wrong way. Anything could trigger him.

The last thing I see before I go for help is Dad dragging Mum around the room by her long plait. She caught my eye for a second, her face wracked with fear and probably pain, her eyes beseeching me for help. And then I was off, running up the steps as fast as I could, crossing the road and plunging back down the steps on the other side to get help from the Pakistani neighbour.

This is one of my first memories: five years old, running fast, trying to save my mum.

That day, I had found some neighbours and we all raced back across the street to put an end to Dad's attack. But it would happen again. Dad seemed to have this insatiable need to break Mum's spirit – and he did this with his fists.

As the youngest of a big family back in Pakistan, Mum had been cherished and encouraged to speak her mind. When she moved to Bradford to live with her new husband, even though she had no English and was just seventeen, she still thought her opinion was worth something. She had a streak of confidence that Dad clearly felt he had to beat out of her.

I would add other incidents of abuse to this first recollection. One that stands out in my memory is notable for the momentary disbelief it ignited in my young mind. I was in the kitchen of our house on Hartman Place. We had just eaten a big meal Mum had prepared for our extended family. She was sitting in a chair and holding little baby Imy in her lap. I was standing beside her as she chatted with the other adults, when one of the men on my dad's side of the family suddenly lunged out and struck Mum hard across the face – because she dared to disagree with him. I felt the shock of the impact, both of us jolted by the blow. But I wasn't scared for myself. It was Mum who'd taken the punch, and I was terrified for her. The man had landed one strike before another member of the family intervened and it was over. It was never discussed, and I never challenged my mum about what had happened – somehow knowing instinctively not to ask.

Was this right? I had wondered. Was my mum so disobedient than *anyone* could hit her whenever they felt like it?

It was by no means an isolated incident. I became increasingly aware of other male members of the family lashing out at Mum whenever they perceived she had stepped out of line. Did other women in the family receive the same treatment for similar 'infractions'? No. Just my mum. And my dad, by never intervening, had given his tacit approval. He might as well have announced to the world: *Step up, step up, one and all – hit my wife, she needs the discipline.*

If my mum's dad was visiting from Pakistan and witnessed the violence, he'd try to intervene. But as a visitor, and therefore a 'guest' of our family, he couldn't do much. His protestations were ignored in any case. His view was that Mum was now Dad's responsibility and it was up to him and his family to 'reprimand' her. He believed that whatever goes on in a marriage must be endured; that once a woman makes her vows, she only leaves her husband's house once she's dead. So Mum had no choice in the matter – she had to put up with it. Her own parents wouldn't have welcomed her home. This thinking stems from the long-held cultural belief that our daughters never truly belong to us – they are only being raised by us until the day they are betrothed and 'handed over' to a man and his family. A daughter is a gift to be cherished – until her rightful owner claims her, so to speak.

My grandfather's advice to Mum? 'Hold your tongue and

no one will hit you.' She was being silenced. That, in his mind, was the only way he could save her.

We were intertwined as a large family in ways that many white families might not recognise. Marriage to first cousins is common in Pakistani culture; it goes back to traditions of land ownership within rural communities. When you marry, you become part of a very close-knit community.

My mum's brother was married to my dad's sister, and my mum's dad – my grandad – was the brother of my dad's dad, my other grandfather.

None of that explains why Mum bore the brunt of male violence, but I don't doubt that some of it can be traced to these interweaving family connections.

My dad's mother – my grandmother – fell from favour in my grandfather's eyes when he married again. Given it was legal to marry multiple times in Pakistan, it was also legal to have more than one wife in the UK, as British law recognises the laws of other countries when it comes to marriage. He married his second wife in Pakistan, applied for a visa and brought her over. He now had a new bride to cherish – and my grandmother could do nothing about it.

This second wife was Mum's cousin. And while it wasn't uncommon back then, nobody likes a second wife in my culture. My dad didn't like it and nor did his brothers. It wasn't a leap to think that maybe some of the abuse Mum suffered was a form of retribution for this marriage. But, at the same time, I don't think that cycles of violence – wherever they occur – can ever be fully explained, let alone justified. My grandfather, meanwhile, enjoyed the best of both worlds, maintaining two households and two wives for the rest of his life.

My fight to be visible began with my conception.

For the first twelve months of my life, my dad wouldn't look at me – let alone hold me. He was so disappointed that I'd been born a girl, he literally couldn't bear the sight of me, even though he bore half the responsibility for my gender. My battle began before I was born.

Dad would play with the baby boys in the extended family, deeply wounding my mother. Mum was so upset that one day she held me out of the window: 'If you can't even look at your own daughter then we might as well let her fall to her death,' she told him. When Mum became pregnant again straight after I was born and gave birth to a baby boy who died within hours, her big brother – my uncle Iqbal – chided Dad, pointing out that this was God's way of telling him to treasure me. By giving him what he wanted – a boy – and then snatching him away, God was telling Dad to love the child he already had.

That was the day my dad fell in love with me.

And I truly loved him back. Even though I had seen with my own eyes what he was regularly doing to my mum, I adored him.

As children we live our lives in the present. I never made the connection, at such a young age, that this man was a brute; he was the loving father who bought me sweets and sang to me. I loved how he let me have play fights with him. Even when I accidentally winded him during our horseplay and Mum came rushing in, saying, 'What have you done?

What have you done to your dad?' – Dad just laughed and clutched his tummy. 'It's all right, it's all right, it's just my little Naseem. She's a fighter.'

I didn't understand the violence and perhaps as a little kid I thought that this was just a part of life – just like my mum and dad loving me was a part of life.

Putting me up on my TV pedestal, twirling me round and round, laughing and singing.

Brown girl in the ring, tra la la la la.

My dad, that lovely man who treasured me, was about to bring disaster into our lives.

Even though I was just six years old, the memory of being bundled into the back of a car with Mum and little Imy is still raw and vivid. Mum was pregnant with my sister, Fozia, at the time and our clothes – stashed into bin liners – followed us into the car. We were headed to Kirkham Road, the home of my paternal grandfather, where we were to live from that point on. We had no other option, nowhere else to go, as Mum's parents lived in rural Pakistan.

Dad was one of the few men in the street who owned a car and, ever helpful, he would regularly take the teenage daughter of a fellow neighbour to school. There was gossip at the time that he was having an affair with the mother of the girl, due to his frequent visits to their house. But when Mum confronted him, he denied it.

He was telling the truth.

Shortly after this denial, Dad disappeared – with the neighbour's sixteen-year-old daughter.

I don't think Dad could have chosen a more shocking,

more publicly shameful transgression to blow up our lives. He lit the blue touchpaper and stood back to see what would happen.

Your dad goes off with the neighbour's daughter – their sixteen-year-old daughter – well, that's going to cause a ruckus in any community, anywhere in the world. But it was especially explosive in our case, because Dad had smashed apart the unwritten rules of izzat.

Of Arabic origin, izzat is one of the founding secular principles of British Pakistani life. It is the means by which an individual and his or her family maintain reputation and honour within the community. Honour within the northern Indian, Bangladeshi and Pakistani communities is essential in order to demonstrate an upstanding existence. This principle applies across religions as well as regions, including Hindu, Muslim and Sikh faiths worldwide. Izzat sets the parameters of decency and expectation; it's the glue that holds our community together. Hold true to your izzat and you can hold your head high. Izzat drives you to succeed. The more successful you are, the more izzat you acquire.

But izzat is also about patriarchy – about how men are held in higher esteem than women. It may be the glue that holds people together, but it's also fundamentally about biology: the fact that I was born a girl meant that Dad felt entitled to his hostility towards me.

Dad had compromised his own izzat because he had shamed another man – the teenager's father – not because he had shamed his wife or that sixteen-year-old.

I know. It's complicated.

But patriarchy, sexism, discrimination against women –

every culture in every country suffers from these prejudices. I experience them daily within the elegant confines of Westminster.

The culture in which I grew up clings to those concepts as dearly as any other.

Dad brought shame to our family. He brought a sense of outrage to our neighbour's family. He dishonoured us all. It would be reasonable to assume that the entire focus of the blame would be directed at him. But not so fast. In our community, at that time, it was the women who bore the shame of dishonour when izzat was breached. And so it was my mum – and the girls of the family – who really suffered.

There's a well-known phrase, originating in Pakistan: *When a boy is born, the walls will tremble; when a girl is born, the walls are joyous as they know they will at least be clean.* What a legacy.

We were on lockdown. My dad was being hunted. His life was in danger.

We were bundled off to Kirkham Road initially to escape the threat of retribution from the girl's family. In the days following Dad's disappearance, chaos reigned. Our family's izzat was in ruins. Taking off with someone's daughter was the biggest scandal to hit our community in years and years.

Beyond the Wild West movies of the fifties and sixties, bounty hunters were very much alive and violently kicking in our community. This was 1980, almost the twenty-first century, yet certain people would, for a sum, be happy to find and return your errant daughters – daughters who had run away to escape arranged marriages or just their families.

If a girl had run off with a boy, he could expect a beating. At that time there was an entire police department established to help these women with new identities to evade their desperate, and dangerous, families. These women had jeopardised the household's izzat, and parents, uncles and grandparents would stop at nothing to get it – and their daughters – back.

With the shaming of our neighbour's daughter, there was a genuine fear that revenge would be taken on the younger women of our family by the girl's relatives: cousins, nieces, daughters and granddaughters.

And then there was Mum, who had to take the brunt of the blame, even though she had been the wronged party. Blame her how exactly? Well, it was believed that Mum drove Dad away by not being 'enough' for him – that he was, in a way, left with no choice but to look elsewhere for happiness and satisfaction. Even though Dad was the one who made the catastrophic decision to abandon his family, it was my mum's responsibility not only to bear the shame of his abandonment but to manage the carnage he left in his wake. It was assumed that men can't be expected to behave impeccably all the time – that the woman must, in some way, have provided the catalyst for such shocking behaviour.

Mum told me, many years later, that both her brothers, who lived in the UK, insisted that because of the shame and dishonour that had been thrust upon them, she should give up *his* children – that Imy and I should be parcelled off to my father's house.

'Give him his kids', she was told. 'We don't want them.' If she did that, then she would receive their support.

And what of me? The little girl who wouldn't ever dance on

top of the TV again? I would be torn away from the mother I loved.

Thankfully, Mum was having none of it. And despite the fact that life was now going to get exponentially tougher, she wouldn't back down. She hadn't made my dad run off with that girl. She hadn't brought shame on the family. She would take care of her own children, she told my uncles – including the little one who was yet to be born. She was adamant about protecting us, about keeping us together as a family. And so it was made clear to her: You've made your bed. You've turned down the terms of our offer. So now you're on your own.

We couldn't stay with our grandfather – there wasn't enough room. And anyway, now that we were the children of a man without izzat, no one wanted us. When Mum refused to give us up, she was ostracised and isolated. Not only that, but she was also held to account for driving Dad away.

By August 1980, five months after we'd left our original home and just six weeks after my sister, Foz, was born, we left my grandfather's house.

Now we really *were* on our own.

Over the next couple of years, the four of us – Mum, me, Imy and little baby Foz – moved fourteen times. We shifted ourselves and our belongings from one damp, rat-infested home to another while Mum was constantly trying to rent better places. Often, we were all living in a single room with rising damp, the loo in the backyard. If we moved to a house, we rarely ever slept upstairs as we couldn't afford to heat it. I never slept apart from my mother and my siblings until I married.

Derby Street, Nuttall Road, Paley Terrace – no sooner had we settled somewhere than we'd be on the move again. Imy and I both developed tuberculosis from the damp, but thankfully Foz avoided it. In the winter months, we'd all huddle together in a bed beside a gas fire. I can still see Mum now, crouched in front of the fire at the end of the bed, muttering to herself while she rocked to and fro in her misery. She kept repeating the same words – a plaintive whisper – asking how things were so bad that she couldn't even afford poison to kill herself.

We had very little contact with the majority of the wider family during those years. Because Imy and I were in and out of hospital with TB, those few relatives still speaking to us had to be vaccinated; they were furious with us for bringing disease into the family. We lived a shameful existence. Whichever way we turned, the parameters of all our lives were defined by shame – by our diminished izzat. Defined by the actions of one man who hadn't even hung around long enough to ensure his children had somewhere decent to live.

Mum was a single parent, cast out of the family and left to cope with the fallout of my dad's disgrace on her own. No one gave a damn that we had to move again and again. She was very much the woman who couldn't preserve the respect of her family, while my father – because he's a man – was gradually allowed back into the fold. And he continued to spin the same narrative: that it was all my mum's fault that she was a single parent.

Many years later, when I confronted Dad about his abandonment of us, he blamed my mother. Never elaborating, just repeating the same tired lines: 'I tried, I really tried with your mum to make it work.' His family blamed the fact that Mum never just 'took' a beating from my dad – she always challenged him. It was her fault, therefore, for answering back. It didn't matter whether she was right or wrong. She should have kept her mouth shut and her feelings to herself.

By the time I was seven years old, I knew I had to be Mum's little soldier.

Imy was three, Foz not even a year old, and Mum still struggled with her English. I had to be on hand to help her understand this complex world that threatened daily to overwhelm her. So I became her mouth and ears, translating for her at the Social Security office while she attempted to claim the meagre benefits that would keep her kids alive. I had to look after her, because she was doing everything she could to look after us. It wasn't even a question or a decision: there was no choice. And I wanted to do it. I loved Mum. She was all I had. The men of Mum's family had abandoned her, so I had to pick up the mantle that rightfully they should have carried. Yes, I was only seven – but there was no one else.

Today, Mum loves Bradford as much as I do. But back then, it was an intimidating city for her, filled with financial and linguistic challenges.

What follows is a defining memory for me, one that perfectly captured her desperate vulnerability and the constant anxiety she harboured for our welfare.

We were on the bus on our way to visit Grandad on Kirkham Road, when the bus stopped on Legrams Lane. Mum panicked. She had lost her bearings.

Where were we?

With the three of us in tow, she burst into tears.

'What's the name of your street?' the bus conductor asked. He wanted to help.

When I told him we needed to get to Kirkham Road, he turned off the engine, stepped out of his cab and onto the pavement and pointed out directions.

'Look, Kirkham Road is just over there. Two minutes' walk.'

Mum was sobbing as she dragged us along, relief and despair dogging our footsteps.

It's a memory in technicolour – an example of the mountain my mum was so determined to climb. She was trying to navigate a bus system she couldn't comprehend, in order to visit relatives who didn't care much for any of us anymore, and she had to make sure that she got her children there safely. That's my mum, though: that's the fierce commitment she made to stay part of a community that wouldn't have cared if she had simply disappeared.

But while Mum was a pariah, we hadn't been totally shunned.

Why did she go and visit my grandfather at all, you might wonder. Mum believes in family, in community – above all else, izzat is about family. If you have elders, you have izzat. If your family isn't talking to you, then you are, by definition, without izzat because you don't have the support of your elders.

Dad, meanwhile, did nothing. He gave us no money. He didn't visit. He was totally absent.

One of the stories told in my family was that Dad was a lavish man when we all still lived together. We were the only ones on the street with a colour TV, a VCR and a car. His business had been doing well. But the problem was that it functioned on verbal contracts and so when he ran off with the neighbour's daughter, he abandoned not only his wife and children but his business as well. Because his brothers were too busy with their own jobs to take care of his, Dad's company collapsed.

At this point, my father turned to dealing drugs – specifically heroin.

His izzat should be very low at this point, right? But that's the other thing about izzat: men tend to bounce back from a lack of it far sooner than women. He was gradually regaining his honour and position in the community, while my mother's honour – and there was little enough of it to start with – diminished even further.

Once, when we were living in two rooms on Derby Street with an outside loo and a bathtub in the kitchen, my dad came to stay – with his new wife. Mum had no say in this turn of events; Dad could appear out of the blue whenever he wanted or needed a room for the night, and she just had to let him in. The place on Derby Street had an upstairs and, as usual, we couldn't afford to heat it, so we rarely went up there. Dad said he would take one of the bedrooms and Mum acquiesced. He was our father, after all – he would always be the father of her children.

I was happy to see him. I still loved my dad and didn't blame him for what had happened to us – not at that point anyway.

And his new, by now seventeen-year-old wife? She had no interaction with us at all. My mum must have hated her.

But the shocking fact about that visit is that I can clearly remember seeing a gun poking out of Dad's coat pocket. That was how dramatically his life had changed.

Word got around the neighbourhood that he had dared to show his face and one night, someone tried to set fire to our house by sticking lit matches through the letterbox. While Dad had been slowly edging his way back into the family fold, the girl's family was not so forgiving. He had taken not only their daughter, but their izzat. There was a price to pay.

We were all asleep when baby Foz began to cough – and cough and cough. Awake within seconds, we saw thick, black smoke billowing around the kitchen. Thankfully, the fire hadn't taken hold.

Despite the shock, the thing Mum cried about for days afterwards was my school coat. It had been bought with a benefits voucher and was two sizes too big so that it would last at least a couple of years. Now it was ruined by the smoke. She knew I wouldn't be given another. Not only that, but the 20kg bag of flour Mum had just had refilled – which would normally see us through the month – was ruined. The chapatis and parathas Mum made from that flour formed part of our staple diet.

Dad must have known that the arson attempt was aimed at him, so he left and never stayed with us again. Maybe the intention had been to kill all six of us. To wipe us all out – including the errant daughter.

I still find it hard to understand why my family wasn't enough for Dad. He had three children and an obedient wife, and a successful business in a city that rated him. He was a winner by all metrics. But somehow it still wasn't enough.

Maybe because his own father's new second wife was my mum's first cousin, Dad got it into his head that Mum's family were somehow responsible for his own mother's trials and tribulations. I never found out if that was the case – but I wouldn't be surprised. I don't know and I don't really need to know. He never spoke to me about it. Not even when I went to see him on his deathbed in 2003.

Dad never expressed any remorse, never uttered a *sorry*. For years, I felt so let down, so hurt by his abandonment. But the pain never seemed to register with him. Eventually, with help from some really fine people, I turned my anger towards him into some of the energy that fuels my politics today. I'm now in my fifties, and while I can assure you that nothing in me has mellowed, the anger is now more fuel than flame. I use it constructively – to take the actions I need to support the people I represent.

Survival teaches you something you can't learn any other way. It teaches you resilience.

I know that losing my school coat and our flour to the arson attack almost broke Mum. She knew I'd have nothing to keep me warm and she had no idea where to find the money to buy more flour to feed us. But she kept going. We all kept going. We refused to be beaten. Resilience is the gift of survival. It's one of life's most powerful tools: the secret strength you fall back on when the world turns on you. It's the elasticity that lets you bounce back when you've been punched down.

My resilience arose almost entirely from the obligation I felt to support my mum. As I grew older and I learnt more about my faith as a Muslim, I discovered that this resilience had blossomed. Now, through my faith, I understand that it is my personal responsibility to be the best version of myself that I can muster. As my faith instructs: whatever we have been given, it is our duty to make the best of it. I was gifted resilience very early on and now, as I navigate the turbulent waters of politics, I know how to call on it to keep a steady course.

My mum taught me that you can find your strength in your community, even when that community has turned its back on you. Rejected by her brothers, cast out as a fallen woman because she'd been so humiliatingly abandoned, Mum could have gone into a long-term decline. She could have lost us kids, lost herself, lost her way. But she didn't. She's made of steel, that woman.

Yes, she had lost her izzat – but now she was going to get it back. All on her own.

2

Legrams Lane

It was a long, slow journey and she certainly stumbled along the way, but step by step, Mum began to reclaim her identity – a space in which it was her right to exist.

Despite the lack of support from her family, she refused to disappear. She was determined to ensure that the community understood she had a right to be there – that she and her children belonged. Visibility was key and Mum was always the first to step up when there was a community event: a marriage, a funeral, a birthday. *Nehndra* is the Asian tradition of gifting money to the bride and groom at their wedding: if my mum saw that someone had given five pounds, she would try to give ten. Even if that meant she couldn't eat when she got home, she'd make that sacrifice. Nothing has changed since then; if she hears that someone in the wider family has died, she'll say to me, 'We should visit tomorrow. We need to show ourselves, pay our respects.' She wouldn't want to wait a few days – she'd be right there at the front of the line, ready to congratulate or offer condolences. That was what she did back then, and she became known as someone who was always ready to show her support.

Mum began to look for work and managed to secure a part-time cleaning job at our local GP surgery. Her English was still pretty basic, but all the same, she enrolled on a scheme set up by social services whereby people on benefits were rewarded for care work with a £15 voucher. This work involved looking after disadvantaged and disabled kids, and providing respite care for families with disabled children. While writing this, I sat down recently with Imy and Foz and we recalled how little we actually saw of Mum in those early years. She was always going from one poorly paid part-time job to another, scratching together the money to feed and clothe us.

In all kinds of ways, contemporary society is structured to sustain poverty. Too many politicians around the world still don't understand just how easy it is to slip from a stable and secure life into one that is defined by deprivation. Which is what happened to us. There were no maintenance payments from Dad for the care of his three children, and there was no hope of help from the family. We weren't alone in this nightmare; there are moments in people's lives in every country where critical factors – race, class, education, health – intersect, and can plunge anyone into poverty. If America has a particular problem with race, Britain has an equally deep problem with its obsession with class. The poor in Britain receive worse services than the better-off, because our society cushions those who already have more. When you have so little, the foundations of your life are always brittle and susceptible to collapse.

We had collapsed, and Mum was struggling to put us back together.

During those early years, while Mum battled to reclaim her place in society and received little help from those around her, we weren't in fact totally on our own. At various points there were women – effectively outsiders who weren't connected to our family, neighbourhood or religion – who lent us a hand. Whether they were from social services or Mum's friends from outside the community, they were lifesavers for us. White women, Sikhs and even my old dinner lady (who took me on daytrips to the seaside) stepped up. They were kind and helpful women, donating hand-me-downs and reaching out steadying hands to Mum as she attempted to salvage her dignity from the wreckage my father had left behind.

At the same time, the cold shoulder that my mum received from the extended family filtered down through her to me, because the simple fact that my dad had left us was treated as our *family* responsibility.

When I use the word 'community', I'm referring to the Asian community – the people we'd come across as we went about our day-to-day lives. As I've mentioned, there are two big occasions in the Asian community: death and marriage. Culturally, we are a very tight-knit group and the giving and receiving of gifts forms a significant part of our culture. While Mum continued to use these events to maintain contact with people in her community, they never afford her the respect of a married woman. Despite her efforts to claw it back, her izzat had all but vanished. Mum knew this, of course – and she also made sure that I knew it, too.

Even though our lives had been thrown into turmoil, I was still a child. Occasionally, I would ask Mum for a new item of clothing or a particular haircut, or if I could go to the local park with school friends. In those days, she had a ready comeback: 'You can't have or do that, because you haven't got a father.' She constantly reminded us of our lowly position. Our spirits had to be contained, and me and my siblings were discouraged from being visible.

The framework of izzat and shame dictated how we lived our lives. For example, when I was twelve years old I wanted a fringe – all the girls had fringes. But when I told my mum, back came the usual response: 'You can't cut your hair, because you haven't got a father.' This blunt comeback obviously requires a bit of unpacking. A hairstyle is a fashion statement; if you have a style that's on the fashionable side, it's assumed that your father has given his consent for such a bold move. This patriarchal consent permits a little digression from the norm. Now, if you don't have a dad and you have a cool haircut, you're not accorded the same concession. Your haircut has not been sanctioned and therefore you are a *loose* woman. There is no one overseeing your behaviour, and that path will lead to your downfall. So you aren't just being judged for the way you look now, but where you will end up.

Not having a father meant that me and my siblings had to toe the line of respectability with diligence. And if I did anything wrong, it would be, *Well, that's what happens when you don't have a father.* I wanted to wear trousers because I was quite the little tomboy when I was a kid. But it was the same response again: 'Nope. You haven't got a father to give you his permission.' I began to be defined, and the limits of my life set, by the terrible error I'd made in losing my dad.

In Islam, the definition of an orphan is a child who has lost their father before puberty. It's important to note that Islamic culture is very sympathetic and generous to orphans, but in my case, I'd somehow become responsible for my father's absence. This isn't about Mum holding me responsible in any way, but about us as a family having to pay the price for Dad's irresponsibility. This was about the repercussions of his abandonment, and those included having to behave like an angel so no one would point a finger at us and shake their heads at our lack of respectability.

I'd work tirelessly against all these seemingly tiny microaggressions for days – even weeks – eventually exhausting Mum so she'd let me have that fringe, wear those trousers. I knew, without being able to define it and even though I was shamed every day of my life by the knowledge of it, that it couldn't really be my fault that I didn't have a dad. And in fact I knew I *did* have a dad – wasn't I his 'brown girl in the ring' after all? I just didn't seem to have one any longer, and everyone seemed to think that was my fault and Mum's fault. But that little flame of independence, which maybe Mum lit for me when I was born, that little flame made me refuse to accept that this was how it must be.

I was never allowed to forget, and neither was Mum, that honour belonged to men, and women were responsible for the shame. This mindset has shifted somewhat today, and the emphasis has moved on from the cultural definition towards a more Islamic definition. From an Islamic perspective, you are not supposed to force your daughter into marriage. Your son and daughter are equal and, if anything, your daughter ranks a little higher because of the status women enjoy. For me, my religion has been liberating in that way. These days, the family's izzat is defined by the legacy their kids create by being the best they can be, instead of following an arcane definition of how to conduct yourself. We still have a long road to travel – I'm not saying things are perfect – but attitudes are definitely changing.

It was the early 1980s and in Britain, Margaret Thatcher was driving her home ownership agenda with the Right to Buy scheme. The vision she was selling was a future in which families could achieve freedom and independence by buying the council house they were living in. It was a beguiling dream for many working-class families around the country and it's no surprise that its impact inspired Mum as she fought to restore her izzat. She decided that somehow or other, after two years of renting temporary lodgings in one damp, cramped place after another, she would find a home that we could call our own.

Mum worked out that if she sold all the jewellery she'd been given on her wedding day, she would have enough money to put down a deposit to secure a mortgage. Finally, she would have a place of her own – and somewhere she could eventually pass on to her children. While in some ways it saddens me that Mum felt she would regain her respectability by going down this route, I can understand her reasoning. In those days, many people were seduced by the tempting dream of home-owning independence – though for some, that dream turned out to be more of a nightmare, as they found themselves in debt, struggling to make the monthly mortgage payments. There was an added dimension to Mum's desire to own her own home: her brothers had houses and she wanted to show them that despite the fact that they had abandoned her, she was going to survive nonetheless, and, like them, she would be a homeowner in her own right.

But there was one problem with her plan – without a full-time job, Mum couldn't apply for the mortgage in her own name. So she went to her brothers, both of whom were self-employed. The mortgage she was after was tiny to modern eyes: only £5,000. The house itself was only worth £10,000. She suggested to my uncles that if one of them put the mortgage in his name, she would make sure all the payments were made until it was fully paid off. These were the same brothers who had insisted Mum hand her children over to Dad, so maybe it's no wonder they both refused to help her. Not very financially savvy, they were also scared of any potential tax implications. The irony is that the Asian community is so tight-knit – like I said, it looks after its own – but no one had our backs.

Next, my mum went to my paternal grandad for help, and he came up with an alternative proposition: he would buy the property and we could live in it for a few years until his eldest son from his second marriage came of age. At that point, we'd need to leave and the property would become his son's.

Mum was about to accept this proposition – after all, a semi-secure home was better than moving from one dump to another – when one of her neighbours pointed out that in five years' time she'd back where she started: homeless and with nothing to show for her initial investment. It wasn't a generous offer, it was exploitation.

My mum was still in her twenties, her English was very poor; she had no profile within the system, no credit rating, no regular employment and no husband. The odds were stacked against her. She could see that her neighbour was right, but what other option did she have?

That's when the same neighbour made the fateful suggestion, 'What about my nephew Azam? He'll help you.'

Ah, if I had a superpower, I'd reel back the years and return to that very moment and whisper into Mum's ear, *No, Mum – do anything, but please, please, not this. Forget about owning a home. Me and Imy and Foz, we don't care about moving around. We love you and we love each other and we want to be happy. Put your name down on that housing list, we'd be so content in a little council flat. Honestly. We don't need you to buy us a house. Please, don't do it.*

'Uncle' Azam, as Imy, Foz and I came to know him, appeared to be a successful, married British Asian businessman. He had his own cash-and-carry store and he seemed like the generous, community-oriented type. He was already a familiar face because, aware of Mum's financial circumstances, Azam would often pick up a bag of fruit from his shop and drop it off at ours when he visited his aunt. Was it inappropriate that he should be visiting this single mum with gifts for her children? Not really. And Azam was kind to me and my siblings; he smiled a lot, patted our heads and gave us sweets. We liked him.

Today, his attention would look a lot like grooming. Today, we'd look at the isolated, 24-year-old mother struggling to raise three young children on her own and we'd wonder why this guy was hanging around. Today, Mum would be considered vulnerable as she negotiated insecure accommodation, grinding poverty, language barriers and kids suffering with TB. But back in the 1980s, Azam was deemed a good Muslim man, attentive to those in need, his izzat wholly intact.

Azam just wanted to help us out, the neighbour reassured Mum, and this is what he would do for her. Mum would put down the deposit on the house by selling her jewellery. The property would be registered in Azam's name, because Mum couldn't qualify for a mortgage, and Mum would make the regular payments via Azam until the mortgage was fully paid off. At that point, Azam – our knight in shining armour – would transfer the property back to Mum and everyone would be happy. We were still living in two rooms of a back-to-back in those Bradford streets, and all Mum wanted was to provide us with a permanent home and, eventually, long-term security. To her, this was a chink of light at the end of the long, dark tunnel her life had become.

It made sense in other ways, too. Our family, the Shahs, are also known as Syeds – a genealogical line of Muslims that traces itself directly back to the Quraish, the tribe of the Prophet Muhammad, peace be upon him. Syed women are viewed as the mothers of the *Ummah* – the community of believers in Islam, including those who have converted to the religion rather than being born into the lineage. Syeds are held in high esteem by the wider Muslim community, and marrying outside the lineage is frowned upon.

How does this esteem manifest? For starters, the community holds higher expectations of our behaviour. Whereas baradarism is about wealth and power, Syeds are seen as a cut above because of their bloodline and the responsibility it carries. This status has very little to do with wealth – it's more about upholding the name.

Part of Dad's downfall in choosing the neighbour's daughter

was that she wasn't Syed, so he heaped insult upon injury by leaving his Syed wife for a non-Syed girl.

Syeds consider themselves to be from a 'pure' family line, which is something to be proud of. It would be fair to ask how this status benefitted my mother – if she was a Syed, shouldn't she have been given the benefit of the doubt where Dad was concerned? But this is where it gets tricky. The goalposts are different for Syeds. In order to honour your illustrious bloodline, you must strive to be better than your neighbour. Held to a higher standard and a finely tuned moral code, a Syed should lead an exemplary life and become a role model or leader. In many ways, Mum's Syed status was a disadvantage when her life fell apart, because her fall from grace went deeper. Ironically, she might have fared better if she had been born of a less illustrious lineage. That my father had abandoned us so publicly and so spectacularly was *her* downfall. As a Syed woman, she should have been able to keep her husband. Izzat once again shows itself as a double-edged sword: there's the honour associated with being a Syed descendant, but whatever you might achieve in life – however successful you are – it's still seen as nothing more than what's expected of you. Your success, however huge, is just the fulfilment of your birth right. Anything less than that and you're letting down the Pakistani community. And if you have the temerity to have your husband abandon you for the sixteen-year-old neighbour, then what hope is there for you in the community? It's ten times worse *because* of your bloodline.

While I try to live by the principals of my lineage, I don't, for a second, subscribe to the idea that one bloodline holds superiority over another.

LEGRAMS LANE

*

The house Mum wanted to buy – and that Azam said he'd help her buy – was in Legrams Lane in Bradford, not far from other streets where we'd spent the last couple of years moving through temporary accommodation. But Legrams Lane was a cut above Derby Street and Nuttall Road, partly because a number of Syed families had houses nearby, but mostly because it had an internal toilet – a proper bathroom. A decent terraced house, it was very different from the rental places we'd lived in over the years.

Mum would be in her own home and living among other Syeds. Even though we could never be properly respectable – because of course we didn't have a dad, and Mum didn't have a husband – she could still hold her head up and know that she was at least looking after her own among other Syed families.

And so, a new chapter began. We had a home. Our days fell into the kind of routine we craved. When me and my siblings returned home from school, we'd have tea together before Imy would go off to the madrasa in the mosque every night, where he would deepen his understanding of our religion.

My faith as a child wasn't what it is today. Back then, my understanding of Islam was largely cultural. Of course, I knew God existed – fear of God had been deeply instilled within me. The stories I was raised on were brutal and absolute: if you steal, you will lose a hand; if you lie, your tongue will be cut out. Add in the fires of hell that awaited me on the Day of Judgement – should I stray from the prescribed and narrow path of obedience – and you have a child who sees God as vengeful and intolerant. There was no talk of His mercy, His benevolence or His forgiveness. There was no spiritual dimension at all – just fear and retribution.

I would have had little opportunity to learn more about my religion, even had I been so inclined, because only boys could attend madrasa. My own religious education took place at a neighbour's house, where I was obliged to learn Arabic in order to read the Qur'an. Yes, I could read Arabic fluently – I still can – but I had no idea what any of the Arabic text I was so diligently reciting actually meant. There was no English translation of the Qur'an in our house at any point.

Today, there are countless classes attended by children and adults to study the Qur'an and learn about the life of the Prophet Muhammad, peace be upon him, and what it means to be a Muslim today. Above all, we are encouraged to understand the meaning of our sacred book and prayers.

To be able to make her mortgage payments to Azam, Mum was still working as a cleaner for the local GP surgery and also looking after disabled kids until their parents returned from work. Occasionally, she would leave me and Imy to look after Foz. It was around this time that my grandmother began to visit more regularly from Pakistan so she could help out. It was also to be the beginning of Foz's extended trips back to Pakistan with my granny – trips that would continue for the next ten years.

My grandmother was a very interesting character. She was a hard woman who'd had a hard life, but she could also be warm and funny.

My grandfather once belonged to the merchant navy, and he was usually posted in Myanmar, then known as Burma.

When it was time for him to marry, a suitable wife was presented to him. Soon after he was posted abroad, his bride – left alone for years at a time – abandoned the marriage and returned to her own family. This was to happen several times, until it was decided that his next (and hopefully final) marriage would be to a widow with her own daughter. She wouldn't expect too much from him and would count herself lucky that a man wanted to marry her, given the burden of her widowhood and single-parent status. This widow was my grandmother.

It was easy to see where my mum got her feistiness, and I suppose I inherited the same from her. My gran had a strong work ethic. Back home in Pakistan, she managed the crops and livestock along with the rest of the family. I guess I was a little scared of her – she could be brutal in her criticism, sharp-tongued, sarcastic and fond of swearing. But at the same time, I felt a deep respect for her. In the evenings, I loved to watch her settle down by our gas fire and enjoy a few tokes from her hookah pipe. She had a sadness about her, too – both her sons had been sent away to England at the age of ten to receive an education and a better life than she could offer them in the village.

My grandmother's visits – because she was an elder, a respectable woman and a Syed – gave us back some of the izzat that had been sorely lacking in our household since my dad abandoned us. Her priorities weren't so much about helping out around the house, or with us children, as they were about supporting Mum and showing some solidarity now that she was a single mother.

Mum began to try to build more bridges with the family

that hadn't stood by her. Even though many of her in-laws had abused her in the past, she would still invite them and their families over for tea. She would also cook for our neighbours. She would do anything to establish herself, in her eyes, more firmly within the community. She craved acceptance.

The house in Legrams Lane didn't just represent security to my mum. It represented everything about her life that she had lost when my dad left us. Sometimes, events and objects take on a meaning beyond their physical presence. This wasn't just a little terraced house in a street in Bradford, which in 1983 cost £10,000. It was a sanctuary. It was where we would not only be safe and secure, but where our futures could begin to take shape. Mum was clawing back her respectability, and the house was the first step on the road to recovering her izzat.

The day Azam took Mum to the house in Legrams Lane, after he'd been handed the keys by the estate agent, was the day he raped her for the first time. In the house that was purchased with the deposit paid for by the sale of her wedding jewellery – the house she thought was going to be hers, to be ours – was the very same place where her utter vulnerability was exposed. She crossed that threshold full of optimism for a new start and a better future, but she quickly discovered the terrible price she was to pay.

Despite the horrific abuse Mum suffered at the hands of Azam, she never stopped clinging to the hope that this was the only way to offer us the security she believed we desperately needed. A home in which we could thrive, a house to grow up in. But the true cost to her would prove to be far more than any of us bargained for.

3

A Respectable Businessman

I was ten years old when we moved into the new house in Legrams Lane. Despite the fact that we were now, superficially at least, a more 'respectable' family, because we lived in our own home in a street where other Syed families lived, we were still the odd ones out. Because, yes, of course: we didn't have a dad and Mum didn't have a husband.

We would never be able to shake off that stigma and I would bristle inwardly every time a neighbour or an aunty or anyone at all would make a comment designed to sting me where it already hurt.

'Are you sure you should be out at this time, Naseem? Oh, I guess it's because you don't have a dad to tell you any better.'

'Naseem, shouldn't you be at home reading your Qur'an? Given you haven't got a father, you should be praying, not playing in the streets like this.'

Endless, exhausting criticisms about some fault in my character – a fault that I had little hope of correcting – plagued my life.

Perhaps these snide comments made me less sympathetic or attuned to Mum's circumstances than I could have been. When I would tell her how kind Uncle Azam had bought me sweets from his cash-and-carry, and how it was nice to have a good man around who me and Imy and Foz could look up to, she never really engaged or responded. She was always exhausted. She was exhausted from running from one badly paid job to another and trying to do her best by her kids, all the while trying to find time to appease the community. Sometimes I resented her for it – for her lack of attention. I couldn't understand why she was spending so much time looking after those disabled children and not at home with us.

I had a couple of white friends – Michelle and Joanna – who went to Waverley Middle School with me. They seemed to have what appeared to me to be 'normal' lives. Their mums didn't work as hard as mine, their dads came home after finishing work, and they would all sit down to tea together. In my home, it was me who often prepared our tea. There was no sign of a dad in my house and instead a man who we weren't related to would occasionally visit with bags of sweets or fruit, before leaving again. That was my 'normal'. We never went on holiday as a family, although, as I've mentioned, one of the dinner ladies at my school, Mrs Brassley, who was aware of our dire financial situation, took me with her on her family holiday to Scarborough and on occasional daytrips.

Joanna was a tomboy, and my closest friend at the time. I'll never forget her pride in the small pool table her parents gave her for her birthday. A pool table! I had a similar revelatory experience when we visited a friend of my mother's whose daughter, Parveen, had her own bedroom, the walls of which were covered with posters of Boy George. I had no posters and I shared a bedroom with my mum and siblings. We had to save on heating where we could and sharing a bedroom made the most sense. While I loved Wham! and Culture Club, it would never have crossed my mind to put up a poster. Our bedroom was about function – it was a place to sleep, not to express my popstar crushes.

The first time Joanna came to my house after school, a neighbour told my mother that she had seen me invite a white boy into the house – Joanna's hair was short.

While I was certainly aware of the differences between me and my white friends, I didn't attach too much significance to them. These differences felt part of the landscape of my childhood. Joanna was from a white working-class family, I was from a poor Asian background, and that was just the reality. I never wanted what she had, because, culturally, we were worlds apart.

The strong contrast between my school and home environments took a little navigating, but mostly I moved seamlessly between the two. I had a perfect attendance record despite the fact that we were always on the move.

My attendance record had a lot to do with the fact that I loved school and, despite our obvious challenges, I did well in my exams. School provided a constant in my chaotic life. And because we all wore uniforms, I never had to worry too much about keeping up with the fashions.

Even so, I was a strong-willed child, a bit of a tomboy, a bit of rebel. I was the child who had wanted that fringe, despite the fact that I never had a dad. Rather than feeling sorry for myself, I was getting angry. It wasn't our fault that he had left us, but it was becoming increasingly clear to me that we were carrying the burden.

*

Azam's sister lived two doors down from our house and how could they not have known what was going on? Not that he was regularly assaulting Mum, of course, but it's hard to believe that they didn't suspect she was in a relationship with him. Azam appeared every two or three days, and to my young eyes, he seemed like he cared for Mum. He was always joking around with her, and to me he could do no wrong. He gave me the attention I craved – that's why I called him Uncle.

He may have been a respectable businessman, store owner and all-round white knight, but Azam Mohammed wasn't all that he seemed. He was a drug dealer, for a start – those treats he lavished upon us must have been paid for with the profits he made from selling heroin.

The first time Azam raped Mum – in her new home – he made it clear to her that she would be required to make herself available to him whenever he wished. That was the deal that came with the house. From that day on, he would assault her at his leisure.

My mother had lost two babies: a baby boy, Shah, just days after he was born in 1974 and before I had even laid eyes on him, and a baby girl, Parveen, in 1975. Shah had heart problems and Parveen had other serious health concerns. I remember wishing that my baby brother had lived. As a young child, I wanted to become a heart surgeon so that I could save babies like Shah. I carried that dream with me for years.

Azam had taken Mum to visit her dead children's graves in Bowling Cemetery, where he raped her after she had refused to act as his drug mule, transporting heroin into the UK from Pakistan. This was just one of the many scenes of Azam's brutal abuse of my mum. In her desperation to hang on to her home and provide a secure, warm and comfortable base for her children, Mum bore his attacks in silence.

In those days, Zoora Shah – my mum – was always on the go. I don't remember her ever sitting down to watch TV with us. It was very important to her that we all ate together – we'd share plates of curry and big piles of chapatis – but we never had fun days out. We never went food or clothes shopping together either; Mum did all of that on her own. I don't remember her being particularly affectionate with us. She was constantly preoccupied and visibly stressed. Mum's way of showing love towards her children was practical. Looking back on it now, I'm not sure that she had the capacity to do anything more. Now that I'm a mum myself, I try to be both practical *and* affectionate. I cuddle up with my kids. We're tactile, we watch movies and we fight over the popcorn. My own emotional intelligence was forged through adversity – I want my children to be smart and astute, but I don't want them to suffer the same adversity.

However, Mum's love language was all about security. It wasn't about physical affection, but rather physical care. We were never hungry, our bodies and clothes were always clean and, albeit fragile, we always had a roof over our heads. Often this came at great expense to herself, yet later I was to learn that Mum never considered packing us all up and leaving Legrams Lane. Not only did that house provide us with the security she was desperately trying to give us, but she was terrified to leave, because she knew that Azam would track her down if she did. He saw her as his possession and would have put every effort into finding her if she absconded. His trump card, however, was the house. He controlled her because, legally, he owned our home – and he would have thrown us all out if Mum put a foot wrong.

In the wider community, people assumed Mum was Azam's mistress because he treated our house as his own, freely visiting whenever he wished. What little respect she had clawed back by moving into her own home in a Syed neighbourhood was gone. Our neighbours and extended family believed Mum had choices – and she had made all the wrong ones. If we were outcasts before Azam came on the scene, we were even more toxic now.

As the months passed, Mum became visibly more distressed. She was snappier than usual with us and always preoccupied. If she hoped for a little respite when Azam was arrested and imprisoned for drug dealing, she was disappointed. He insisted Mum visit him in prison, tacitly implying that there would be repercussions if she didn't accede to his every whim. And so, off Mum and I went. I was eleven years old, still Mum's loyal lieutenant and translator.

We sat down with Azam and he and Mum talked while I looked around the room. As I was eyeing up all the other inmates, my gaze landed on a man who looked very familiar.

Wearing identical prison scrubs to Azam, he was the same good-looking guy he had been when he had left us, his hair as full and thick as ever. I couldn't believe what I was seeing: it was my *dad*. And there was his new wife, sitting across from him at their own table. I didn't dare to get up and approach them without Mum's permission, but something told me not to interrupt her rather intense exchange with Azam.

I wondered whether this was what happened to all the men I thought were my protectors. Did they all have to end up in prison? Maybe there was something about me that invited these dark turns of events. And it was probably the same thing that had driven Dad away. Later, I was to discover that he, too, had been put away for drug dealing.

I had been a daddy's girl growing up, the apple of his eye, so that day I was happy to see him. Equally, I was reluctant to leap off my chair and run into his arms – hadn't he left us after all? Hadn't he hurt us all so badly? I was confused, angry, upset – yet pining for a hug. I also understood that, given Dad was with his new wife, I wouldn't have been welcome in his arms anyway. We were the family he had cast aside; he had no room in his life for his children.

In the end, I didn't point him out to Mum. Afterwards, on the way home, I didn't even mention it.

It was during one of these visits that the abuse Mum endured escalated. Azam, a drug-dealing rapist who was enjoying certain privileges in prison – cigarettes, extra food – had to pay for these favours, and the only way he could do this while incarcerated was to pimp out my mother.

Mum sent me off to the vending machine so I wouldn't hear him explaining to her that she would soon be receiving visits from criminal associates of his, and that she should be 'nice' to them. By *nice*, he meant sex. These random strangers would be expecting to have sex with my mum whenever they wished.

In my mother's eyes, she had no choice. The threat was always that she would lose the house – and if that happened, her sacrifice would have been for nothing. She had given her all for our security and she wasn't going to give up now. Now she was finally a homeowner, the house was symbolic of the little dignity she had remaining.

What could she do? Who could she go to for help? She couldn't go to her family: having blamed her for my dad's desertion, they would hardly reach out to her now that she was, to all intents and purposes, behaving even more disgracefully, more shamefully than before.

Who else could she tell? The police? Well, she did try. Driven to despair, she went to the police when yet another 'friend' of Azam's turned up at the house, expecting to have sex with her. She somehow managed to lock this stranger in her bedroom, then ran the three hundred yards to the police station to ask for help. When she returned with an officer, the man had escaped and the matter wasn't pursued. No one took her seriously. Azam was still in prison when this happened – she wouldn't have dared to run for help if he'd been around.

I had no idea what was going on, and neither did Imy or four-year-old Foz. In fact, no one knew. As far as anyone else was concerned, these men were just friends of Azam's. They were just dropping off provisions for the family that had been paid for by their generous and kindly mate, who just wanted Zoora Shah and her three kids to be taken care of. No one could have known that these men were raping Mum while her kids were downstairs doing their homework. No one could hear the hissed threats to her life, the pulling of that beautiful long hair, the secret punches and scratches. This wasn't just a cycle of violence that Mum was caught up in, it was a whirlpool in which she was spinning. She was out of control, alone and unable to call out to a single soul.

Meanwhile, she carried on trying to live a normal life – working, visiting the neighbours who were still talking to her, cooking for us and taking care of us. She was as busy as ever. We never had much money, but there was always food in the house; we never went without. And while we may have longed for new clothes and haircuts, we were never hungry and we never felt our poverty.

To my confused and critical eyes, it seemed to me that Mum was in control of the choices she was making about who she spent time with. And now that Uncle Azam wasn't around, I didn't understand why Mum would still have to hang out upstairs with the strangers who turned up at our door. Why wouldn't she sit down with her children? Were we not interesting enough for her? Were those men such stimulating company?

Once or twice, I confronted Mum. Who were these men? But I was always met with her silent refusal to engage with my concerns.

I was so angry with Mum that I even wrote to my dad in prison, complaining about these 'visitors' to the house. I actually wrote the sentence: 'I know enough about my mum to think that she's a prostitute.'

It's hard to imagine I still had enough faith in my dad to believe he could help us, and yet – just like everyone else – I believed Mum was in the wrong. At eleven years old, I knew my culture well enough to understand that it wasn't normal or right to have boyfriends – or whatever these male visitors were – just dropping by. Azam might have been a respectable guest, but these men were not.

Once, I ran away to my uncle's house – to the brother who had advised Mum to give us up into Dad's care. I told him that Mum was seeing all kinds of men and that we didn't like it. My uncle just sent me home, ignoring all my protestations. He didn't want to know.

It's hard not to look back and imagine whether a simple intervention could have changed all our lives.

Prison services had intercepted the letter I'd written to my dad and a child protection order was raised. Shortly after, I was visited by a social worker who took me out for coffee and a 'chat'.

'Naz, it's not a crime for your mother to see men or have boyfriends,' she told me with a smile. 'She is an adult and a single woman.' Clearly, she viewed me as a devout tweenager who was struggling to accept that her mother had intimate relationships with men.

I never questioned that social worker and I never questioned any of my elders, but I still didn't like it. To cap it all, the social worker was an Asian woman – surely she should have understood that in our culture, you just don't have boyfriends. Why was she trying to convince me that the opposite was absolutely fine?

Mum was living in a nightmare. It must have felt like she was having the life punched out of her every single day. And yet, through it all, she resolutely never told a soul in our community. This poor, lonely woman was being exploited and abused in full view of the world, yet no one raised the alarm.

These days, I think we have developed a better understanding of sexual exploitation and its links with poverty and violence, and both the police and social services are much more attuned to recognising the kind of horrific abuse my mum was suffering. Back then, Mum was simply abandoned. But she must have retained some agency, because she believed that if she could tolerate rape, violence, poverty and the disdain of her community, then her three children would thrive. That was her duty, and it was her love for us that kept her lips sealed.

Occasionally, Mum's instinctive sense of self would try to assert itself and she would tell Azam, either on a prison visit or after another round of abuse at Legrams Lane, that she'd had enough. She was going to tell everyone what a monster he was and expose the vicious truth that lay behind the smooth façade.

'You go ahead,' he'd sneer. 'See if anyone believes you.'

'I will,' she'd repeat. 'I'll do it.'

And that's when he came out with what would turn out to be a fateful phrase.

'Oh, well, Zoora,' he said. 'Just remember, the grass is always greener with that daughter of yours.'

4

From Bradford to Buffalo

'You're going on holiday!'

I'd just turned twelve years old when Mum broke the exciting news to me. I was going on holiday to our family village in Pakistan. Apart from a few trips to Scarborough with my old dinner lady and two brief trips to Morecambe arranged for poor kids by social services, I'd never left Bradford. Now here was my mum, telling me I was going to be flying halfway across the world to stay with her family.

Pakistan was bound to offer more than those miserable days in Morecambe, where I'd had to spend my nights sleeping in a dorm with twelve other girls and my days in wellies and a raincoat because it rained so hard. One day we even went birdwatching. I just didn't get it.

But now, sunshine, family and adventure beckoned!

After the long flight, I stepped off the plane into a world of pulsating heat. I had never felt anything like it in my young life. Could this place really be on the same planet as Bradford? The sky was a deeper blue, the sun more intense, the smells richer – earthy, fragrant and full of life.

The village was a six-hour journey from the airport and to get there I travelled with my aunty Kulsum in my uncle Tasadaq's bus.

'How far is it?' I asked after what already felt like six hours. He pointed to the distant hills. 'That mountain over there,' he told me, with a laugh.

Using an actual mountain to navigate your destination was a new one for me. In the days and months that followed, I was not only introduced to new experiences, ideas and expectations, I was overwhelmed by them.

But right now, on this hot bus that smelled of diesel and which was crammed with passengers – all of whom seemed to be fascinated by this Western child – I was in my element. I felt like a minor celebrity. I didn't pause for breath the whole journey, answering their questions, asking questions of my own. I was fluent in Mirpuri, a dialect of Punjabi spoken in my area of Pakistan, so that made communication easy.

The bus was highly decorated, with horns blaring a melodic jingle as it plunged around steep bends in the mountain road. Not only was the bus packed – often two to a seat, some carrying chickens in baskets on their laps – but there were also people on the roof, tightly gripping the rails as we swayed and swerved, tyres bumping rocks, the horn shrieking, all to the background jingle-jangle of excited voices.

I felt like I'd stepped onto the set of a Bollywood movie.

Soon I would arrive at the home of my maternal grandparents, their children and their grandchildren – a whole community for this child, who was sorely lacking the familial comforts of an extended family. I was to stay with them for three or four weeks, in the tiny rural village of Hamidabad Colony in northeast Pakistan. Or, more correctly, Hamidabad Colony lies in the region known as Azad Kashmir. It's considered a special place – the ultimate familial home to so many people who've embraced the British way of life and who consider themselves British to their core, but whose roots lie in the dusty plains and mountains of this beautiful territory.

The sprawling building where my family lived was in the shape of a horseshoe. It was made up of four rooms on the outer walls and eight across the middle, facing each other across a courtyard. Aunty Kulsum lived with her kids in one corner, while Uncle Tasadaq lived with his kids in another. My grandparents slept in the other corner of the unit. Each room would sleep four to six people on single woven beds known as *charpais* – which in summer might be taken outside onto the veranda or even onto the roof to escape the stifling heat within. On top of these charpais lay a *talai*, a kind of futon mattress that was stuffed with bits of cloth. Every couple of years, a new talai would be made by the village women.

I was used to communal sleeping, but here I was to have my own bed for the first time in my life.

There was one guest room – the *baitakh* – which was used to entertain visitors, and which my grandad used as his quarters. In here, he had a prayer platform where he sat every morning to perform his prayers.

There were three big trees in the garden, two of which produced delicious *shahtoot* berries (extra-long mulberries to you and me). At one side of the courtyard was an area where the livestock was housed – two buffaloes and a donkey. There were also chickens, goats and dogs.

In the room I was to share with my cousin Tahira, my aunty Kulsum and my grandmother, I opened my suitcase to find that Mum had neglected to pack my *churidar* pyjamas!

I loved my churidar pyjamas. Back then, they were the

height of fashion for little girls in Bradford – tight-fitting, colourful and very stylish. I couldn't believe Mum had forgotten to pack them. It would dawn on me soon enough that her packing had been deliberate: Hamidabad Colony was a highly conservative settlement and it was out of the question for young girls to wear fashionable, fitted garments. Mum obviously knew that. Not me, though – I made a scene when I discovered my cherished pyjamas missing, confirming everyone's suspicions that I had become too Western in my ways, too outspoken and altogether too spoilt.

I was proud of my smartest Eid green dress as we walked down the street towards the family home a few days later. It was only when we were inside the house that my cousin told me I needed to change.

'No, Tahira,' I insisted, 'it's my best dress. My Eid dress.' I had enjoyed the day's celebrations – visiting homes in the village to wish everyone *Eid Mubarak* and indulge in the delicious treats on offer. I was a novelty, welcomed warmly into the homes of strangers who stroked my hair and praised my Urdu.

'Look,' Tahira said, pointing to a dark red stain on the back of my dress.

I'd had my first period months ago but had not bled since. I was so ill-informed when it came to the matters of adolescence and the only thing I knew about periods was the nonsense shared among my peers. I had never even discussed menstruation with my mother. Monthly bleeding was a shameful business in my culture and the less said about it the better.

Tahira, a couple of years older than me, told me I had

to change. But I didn't want to – I was enjoying parading through the village in my tailored green Eid suit. When she showed me the blood-red marks on my kameez, I had to agree: it wasn't a good look.

The incident was never mentioned among my family, despite the fact that I had walked through the whole village with blood on my skirt.

The sanitary wear in Pakistan was basic at best: scraps of material folded to make a pad, which were then hand-washed and reused the next time they were needed. But as I was so young, my periods were irregular and I wouldn't have another monthly bleed for eighteen months. For that first year and a half in Pakistan, because I'd had a bleed and then hadn't had any more, I was convinced I was pregnant. And I knew exactly how it had happened. Back home in Bradford, I'd sat next to a boy in class just before I left for Pakistan. That was obviously it – if you sat next to a boy you were bound to get pregnant. That's how little I knew about the birds and the bees, and, as usual, there was no one I could talk to, no one who could explain to me that this wasn't how it worked.

The months passed, my tummy remained flat and I forgot all about it.

Hamidabad Colony was a conservative rural community, a hamlet, not even a village really. There were four streets of houses that backed on to one another – you could easily climb over the roofs to make your way from one house to the next, should you desire. At the end of our row of houses, the land dipped into what we called a *kass* – a valley covered in bushes –

and this is where we went to relieve ourselves. We'd clamber down into the kass, find a bush, do our business, use a stone or leaves to wipe our bums and then return to the house.

At the other end of the village, the land rose up to a steep hill on top of which was a banyan tree. This was a sacred place, known as the Bor. People would climb the hill, say their prayers, tie bits of cloth and flags to the trees and make wishes for the future. They would light lamps and leave sweets as an offering. It was a familiar and comforting sight.

Later, I would make the journey many times myself, leaving a lighted clay pot filled with oil and a wick, and an offering of food. I would tie a piece of cloth to a tree branch and pray that I might go home to Mum and my siblings soon.

But home didn't seem to be on the horizon and before long, all reference to my returning to the UK vanished. I was to be here for a while, it seemed, and Mum wanted me to carry on with my schooling.

The village school consisted of five room-sized buildings arranged around a grassy yard. There were no toilets as such, just the surrounding brushland in which to do our business. We sat in rows on hard, dirt-packed floors, balancing our traditional wooden slates – *dahti* – on our laps to practise our handwriting. Each night, the wooden slate would have to be scrubbed clean and repainted with wet clay so we might use it again the next day. A bamboo stick, shaved to a slant and dipped in ink, was the 'pen' we'd use to practise Urdu calligraphy.

Mumtaz, who ran the school, was studying for an English degree in her spare time, and while all my lessons were in Urdu, I often helped Mumtaz with her homework, enjoying this odd relationship between teacher and pupil while also retaining my English.

Schooling was fairly irregular – by no means every day – but luckily I've always been very good with exams, so I managed to get straight As while I was there. Although I'm a quick learner and am blessed with a terrific short-term memory, it's also worth pointing out that education in rural villages is nowhere near the standard of the British curriculum. I spent my time relearning the topics I was already familiar with, but in a different language.

I was my grandad's favourite grandchild. When, every month, he'd have to visit the nearest town to pick up his pension, he would bring back a special treat of *gulkand*, just for me. Gulkand is a delicious sweet made from fermented rose petals. I was his little *bijili*, his bolt of lightning. Grandad ruled the house and under his supervision, I learnt how to become a villager.

I became a diligent worker and while there was no chore I couldn't master, it was the animals that gave me special pleasure. There were no pets in our household but, very quickly, that's exactly how I came to view the livestock. Hens, buffaloes, goats, dogs, cats. And baby chicks! To pick up a baby chick, which I was desperate to do, I had to isolate its mother under a woven basket, after which I could pet the babies to my heart's content.

My family found my proclivity to ride the donkey hilarious. This animal was the workhorse of the farm, but for a kid from inner-city Bradford a donkey ride was the dream. I even enjoyed milking the goats and buffaloes. The guard dog was a tame creature and to the amusement of all, I would take it on long, rambling walks.

The days were long and the hours filled with tasks that I could never have imagined back home. Here, the whole household would rise at four o'clock in the morning, ready to work. One of my first jobs was to clear up the buffalo poo, after which I would lead these enormous animals to their breakfast. There would be more pooing, more clearing up before they were returned to their grazing land. Nothing was wasted on the farm; I used a shovel and a brush made of the sharp-edged, dry leaves of the local wild grass to scoop the loose poo into a basket of woven reeds, which I'd made myself. When the basket was full, I'd balance it on my head and take it down the street to our manure dump. This dump was an important source of income to the family: every so often, local farmers would stop by and purchase the waste to spread on their land as fertiliser. We'd hang on to the solid turds to use for fuel. These I would squash flat with my palms and lay them out to dry on the roof, in the sun, remembering to turn them regularly. By the following day they'd be ready to use in the fire, so I'd gather them up and give them to Aunty Kulsum, who did most of the cooking.

My buffalo duties done, I would then start the fire and get the tea going. We had two handmade clay stoves in the *dheleez* – the kitchen – an outside room enclosed by a half-height wall. My grandad always liked to have eggs in the morning, freshly laid by the hens we kept, so once the fire was going, I'd put the tea on and pop two eggs into the same pot to boil. Grandad would always be given the first cup, together with his eggs.

The sun was still yet to rise at this point and my grandfather would go off to pray. He was the only member of the household who did pray. While the women read prayers from the Qur'an during Ramadan, it wasn't so different to Bradford, where religion was a cultural rather than a spiritual expression. There was no talk of faith other than to underline all the ways in which displeasing God would result in one punishment or another.

After my morning chores, my aunt would milk the buffaloes while I'd turn my attention to making fifteen parathas. Once I had assembled the dough, I'd cook the flat breads in ghee over the open fire, one for each member of the household.

After the buffaloes had been milked, they needed to be led over to the water tank, which serviced the house. This was the same water tank I scrubbed out every six months. After draining it, I would climb inside and scrub away all the accumulated moss.

Then I would return home to do the washing up, using a bucket of sand and a block of soap. A wet cloth would be rubbed with soap and dipped into sand, which acted as an abrasive to clean the dishes. If any clothes needed washing, I'd use a different block of soap and plunge the dirty clothes into a bucket of water, before scrubbing them clean on a big stone by the water tank.

An absolute rule – one that would result in a huge row, should it ever be broken – was that the buffaloes must never be allowed near the soap. They had a tendency to devour the whole block if the opportunity ever arose. And if they were successful, their milk would be ruined. Normally, the pot containing the soap would be moved out of reach while the buffaloes were being fed. I was very aware of the danger and very diligent in my duties. One day, it was my turn to feed the buffaloes, having made sure to move the soap in its pot out of the way. That afternoon, my aunty accused me of letting the buffaloes eat the soap – she was furious. I insisted that I had removed the pot, so I couldn't be blamed for this disaster. My uncle returned home from work to a terrible atmosphere in the house. Tucked up bed, I listened to my aunt recounting my 'mistake' and expressing her indignation that I wouldn't accept my guilt, that I was too belligerent in my denial. And then I heard his footsteps stomping across the courtyard, all the while grumbling loudly about my disobedience. When he entered my room, I felt his looming presence and then a powerful punch on my back.

Even though he knocked all the air out of my lungs, I never stirred. I just lay completely still, hoping this single almighty blow was all the punishment I would receive.

The next morning, the soap was discovered. No one apologised to me or even acknowledged the incident. And after that punch, I wasn't about to say 'I told you so.'

Another distinct memory of violence from my time in Pakistan happened not long after the episode with my uncle. In the dusty streets outside the compound there were often street vendors selling their wares and their services. Much like ice-cream vans blaring their tunes, these vendors would call out to passing customers 'Come and try this' or 'Nose piercing for your daughters'. It was at this point that my grandmother and aunt decided my nose should be pierced; it was tradition after all. I said I did not wish for my nose to be pierced but no one paid me any heed. I was duly dragged into the middle of the dusty street and held down on the ground, where a thin nail was hammered into my nose. The pain was excruciating; there was no mention of an anaesthetic. To this day I refuse to wear a nose stud.

There was no fridge in the house, so everything was made fresh from scratch every day. We'd all settle down for a siesta in the early afternoon – if it was a school day, I'd be home by 2 p.m. – and after an hour's nap, the dough for tomorrow's breakfast parathas would be prepared and a few of the ingredients for supper would be plucked from the little kitchen garden in the centre of the courtyard. We grew our own coriander and garlic, the rest my aunty would buy from the market. Once we'd all eaten, we'd settle in to watch the daily drama at around 7 p.m. and be in bed by 8 p.m.

On days when there was no school, there would be other tasks such as gathering wood for the fire, or we might head off to work in the nearby field where we grew corn, barley and wheat.

The weeks passed, but Bradford hadn't receded entirely in my thoughts. I held on to the hope that I would go back one day, but I was growing increasingly aware of the distance between my life at home and my life in the village. I tried to believe that however long I remained here, I was still a British teenager.

Despite this, I became a proper villager.

My culture discouraged curiosity in children and when my first month in Pakistan turned into two, then three, no one explained to me why my trip had not only been extended but also showed no signs of coming to an end.

I had very little contact with home and my family. My aunty and uncle and grandparents simply shrugged if I asked when I would be going home. Eventually, I stopped asking.

Pacified from month to month, I just got on with the business of village life. If I did question the length of my visit, I was told that Mum wanted me to stay put, that she wanted me to carry on with my education in the village, and that she would visit soon. Without a calendar or a watch, I could only tell time was passing by the seasons.

Fourteen months into my trip, I went to a wedding and a video of the event was shared with Mum back in Bradford. She thought I looked sad. When she called the village asking why I looked so downcast, she received short shrift from my aunt.

'Do you think you laboured harder than the rest of us that your daughter should receive special treatment?' My aunt viewed my mum's concern as an attack on her care of me. I was constantly made to feel guilty and privileged because I was from the UK and thus luckier than most who had to scrimp a living from the land. If I ever received a gift I was obliged to give it away, because there would be more waiting for me at home.

Contact with home was sporadic. There was only one telephone in the village. If a call came through for a villager, the shout would go out from house to house until whoever was wanted on the phone would scramble over roofs and through gardens to reach the house with the phone. For some reason, calls would be cut off after three minutes, so if a call came through, you had about thirty seconds to get to the phone, leaving you a luxurious two and a half minutes to chat.

When I did speak to Mum, it was so hurried that it often

felt like we hadn't spoken at all. There wasn't enough time to discuss anything meaningful, just a minute or two for Mum to make sure I was well. Even if I had managed to tell her I was unhappy, she would never have dared to challenge her older sister.

Once a month, we'd record a cassette tape, which would be sent back to Bradford with friends or relatives who were travelling between Pakistan and the UK, and they would then deliver Mum's cassette when they returned. The recording was sixty minutes of news, which we'd all listen to together. There was no way I could tell Mum how I was feeling – how I yearned to come home – when there was always an audience on the other end of that tape.

Why was my family so reluctant to send me home? I was the eldest grandchild and they saw it as their duty to discipline me for my wayward Western ways. They were convinced that Pakistan was the place to tame me. At least that's what was communicated to me. I would find out soon enough what they had in store.

It would be two and half years before I was to see Bradford again.

I would only find out much later that Mum had sent me to Pakistan after Azam had made his threat that 'the grass is always greener with that daughter of yours'.

Somehow, she had managed to scrape together enough money to send me away, lest I became his next victim. I can imagine, even in her own misery, the very thought of that must have terrified her and I can, of course, see why she did what she did.

For me, though, once I'd realised I wasn't on 'holiday' – that I had overnight transformed from a Bradford schoolgirl with friends and favourite clothes into a hard- working villager in northeast Pakistan – the world seemed to close in around me. I was a child with no choice other than to obey my elders. The freedom I enjoyed back home was becoming a distant memory. I struggled to recall visits to the cinema with my friends, my school days, the company of my young siblings and sharing family meals. Was that all over, for ever? While I had worked hard to slot into life in my new community – my initial eagerness to engage with the farm resulted in full-time work on the smallholding – I had inadvertently signed up to become a farmer. It had never crossed my mind that my stay here was indefinite.

I had been in Pakistan for two years when Mum came to visit in the summer of 1987, with Foz and Imy. It was lovely to see my mum and my siblings, although Foz had visited Pakistan regularly and for extended periods during the two years I was there. Mum, to be fair, did try to take me home with her after that visit, but my family worked on her guilt, and I had to stay put. Once again, they accused her of not trusting me to their care – a powerful form of emotional blackmail that my mum was in no position to resist. She cared too deeply about my family's approval. I agreed to stay because I didn't want to be the cause of friction between my mum and her relatives. Ever the good little peacekeeper, I was later to discover the real reason for my continued presence in the village.

It was becoming clear to me that I had no agency over my destiny. I had no say in my education or how I spent my time. The control my rural family exerted was total.

The brief sparks in my continued sojourn in Pakistan were my sister's visits. She represented a taste of home and my own family unit. While she was there, we shared my charpai, snuggling close and whispering secrets. (She had been sleeping peacefully beside me the time when my uncle thumped me for allowing the buffaloes to eat the soap, but had remained oblivious.) Foz was my comfort blanket, if you like, and unlike me, she felt totally at home in the village. She was younger and had a different relationship with my grandma, because she had visited so often, the first time when she was just over a year old. There were seven years between us and Foz was seen as the baby of the family. My aunt and grandma adored and spoilt her, feeling sorry that she had never had a father. Foz was an innocent child, whereas I was considered an adult. And a Westernised adult at that.

Before she left, Mum told me that I'd be coming home soon and to just remain patient.

My cousin Tahira, with whom I shared a bedroom, was given extra leniency when it came to work, because her dad had died and she was considered an orphan, just like the Prophet, peace be upon him. She held a certain status in the village, unlike me as someone who had been abandoned by her father.

The definition of colourism is discrimination against people with darker skin, especially within a racial or ethnic group. It was in Hamidabad Colony that I first experienced prejudice based on the depth of my own colouring. Tahira had a delicate bone structure and lighter skin, whereas I had a broader nose, fuller lips and was a shade or two darker than her. According to my elders, who made no bones about it, she was considered pretty and, by comparison, I was deemed ugly. This stigma would follow me into adulthood.

There is an old picture of me and my cousin from that period of my life, standing beside one another in our Eid outfits. We just look like any two young girls posing for a photo – there is nothing exceptional about it. But a relative commented that if you took a closer look, I resembled the hired help and Tahira the child from the revered UK – sophisticated, pretty, fairer. The hired help in our region were dark-skinned and viewed as lower caste.

No one cared that I overheard these comments, or that my darker skin was due to the fact that I played in the sun, whereas Tahira had been conditioned to stay out of the sun to preserve her pale complexion.

I couldn't go home and I was regularly reminded of my privilege, despite the fact I was considered so ugly. Even though my dad had left us, this afforded me little compassion, partly because I was from Britain – a land considered to be full of lucrative opportunities for migrants. I was seen as a lucky Westerner, living a life of luxury. If a family member liked something of mine, such as an item of clothing, I would be expected to give it to them. Mum regularly sent money to my Aunty Kulsum because her children were orphans, as though somehow they were more deserving than us – we who had so selfishly 'lost' our own father.

I thought back to the days of shuttling our belongings from one flat to another and wondered if I had totally misunderstood what the word 'privilege' meant. I certainly didn't feel privileged.

5

Nikah

I was happy playing with my boy cousins on the farm. Having been brought up in Bradford among my male cousins, I had become quite a tomboy myself. When I arrived in Pakistan, there had been some leniency towards my fraternisation with the opposite sex, because I had been raised abroad and was considered a Westerner, so it wasn't entirely my fault. But, bit by bit, I was reined in.

One day, when I was hanging out with my first cousin Mazhar – my uncle's son – Tahira took me aside.

'You shouldn't be playing with Mazhar,' she said.

'Why?' I was confused.

'Because you're going to marry him.'

That was the day I was robbed of my childhood.

I was fourteen years old, and I'd discovered that in due course I would be marrying my cousin. The world never looked the same to me again.

This was the real reason why my family had been so reluctant to let me go. If I returned to Bradford before they locked down our betrothal, I might never return. They simply couldn't take that risk.

Given that no one in my family discussed things like feelings, I didn't talk to anyone about what Tahira had told me. But I felt the obligation to start behaving in a different way.

It's important to note that girl children are never seen as belonging to their family – a daughter is merely raised and nurtured until she is married, after which she will 'belong' to her husband and his family, her rightful 'owners'.

Naturally, I was angry that I couldn't be a normal kid anymore, not now that I was a woman waiting to be wed. The realisation that I would belong to someone other than my mother was horrifying. As was the idea that a life of servitude awaited me. I was powerless to do anything about this new turn of events. I didn't know where my passport was, and I had no money.

My life wasn't my own. Who I met, where I went, how I behaved and who I was to marry – that was all someone else's decision.

Tahira wasn't to escape her destiny either. She was to be married to the son of my mum's cousin Lala Shabbir.

Now that the bombshell had been dropped, my impending nuptials were openly discussed. Every time I mentioned going home to join Mum and Foz and Imy in Bradford, I was made to feel guilty, with cruel digs and sarcastic comments such as, 'I guess we're not good enough for you anymore, Naseem', or, 'Why are you in such a hurry? There's plenty for you to do here.' No one gave me straight answers to my questions, and no one would talk to me about my feelings of homesickness.

The closest I got to a real reason for this marriage to Mazhar was the message that, because Mum had become estranged from her brothers after she refused to give up her children to my dad, the only way to restore unity to the family was for me to marry Mazhar, the son of her brother Tasadaq. Mum hadn't lost her brothers, obviously, but they had disowned her. As usual, we were to blame.

Only in this case, it seemed I could heal the rift. It was up to my family to set things right.

'Your mum has lost two of her brothers already', I was told. 'And now she'll lose this one too. They'll be separated even in death if you don't marry Mazhar.'

Pretty strong stuff for a teenager to contend with, but there was no question of choice. Saying no didn't even cross my mind when there was no good outcome – I jumped either into the fire pit or into the well. We couldn't afford to be further ostracised.

When the suggestion of my marriage was made to Mum, she told the family that she wouldn't lend her support if I was in any way reluctant to take Mazhar as my husband. But Lala Shabbir, Mum's cousin who lived in Luton, went to visit her in Bradford and convinced her that I had agreed to the betrothal.

And this is where the mistake that was to dominate my life for years occurred. My mother's consent arose from the fact that she had been told a lie – that I wanted to marry Mazhar. Given her own disastrous arranged marriage, she would never have forced me into a union I didn't want.

Lala Shabbir then came to Pakistan and told the family that Mum had agreed to the marriage proposal between me and Mazhar. When my aunty told me this, I accepted it. I always did what my mum told me to do – that's how it had always been. So if Mum wanted me to marry Mazhar, then that's what I would do. But on one condition: I needed Mum to tell me herself that this is what she wanted.

So the phone call came, and the shout went up in the village, 'Naseem, phone call!' I leapt across rooftops and sprinted through gardens and finally made it to the phone, all the while painfully aware that the seconds were ticking away.

My exchange with Mum was brief and confusing. But at least I managed to understand that she would support me in whatever decision I made. And I replied that, of course, I would do just as *she* wished. Because it was such an important phone call, other family members had gathered around and the phone was passed from hand to hand without ever coming back to me. As I walked away, all I could surmise was that Mum wanted me to marry my cousin.

She did, however, insist I return to Bradford. I had been away long enough.

A month later, in December 1988, Mazhar and I were joined together in a *nikah* – a binding legal marriage contract in Islamic law. But, given I was only fifteen years old, we would need to renew the nikah the following year when I turned sixteen. At that point, Mazhar would be able to apply for a visa to come to the UK.

Unlikely as it sounds, my most vivid memory of the day I married Mazhar was my makeup.

A local girl had offered her services and, armed with a box full of cosmetics, she began applying layers of colour to my skin. The theory was that the more makeup the better. Bottle-green eyeshadow coated my eyelids, while my cheeks featured two perfect circles of pink blusher. To cap it all, bright red lipstick. That hideous green stays with me to this day. All this on top of my deeply tanned skin. I looked like Wurzel Gummidge's girlfriend, Aunt Sally.

The event itself feels like a barely remembered dream. The ceremony was conducted by the local imam, who asked me three times, 'Do you accept?' From beneath my veil, I replied, 'Yes.' Three times.

The union wasn't consummated, as this wasn't an official wedding but merely the confirmation that we would marry. The nikah was more than an engagement, but less than a formal marriage declaration. I was finally going home, and given that I might change my mind when I discovered how Mum and I had been played off against one another, this arrangement would guarantee my return. Once again, I had no choice – I was as good as married, tied to Mazhar whether we had consummated the marriage or not.

There is no way back from a nikah.

There was no hint of romance between us – we had barely looked at each other during the ceremony – but Mazhar was very happy. He had secured his ticket to the UK.

It was then I began to hope that it would take years for Mazhar to get his visa and join me. By which point, I'd have gained some qualifications and a job, and maybe even bought a house. Who knew where I'd be? It was long enough in the future for me to believe that I didn't have to worry about Mazhar. According to British law, I had to be sixteen years old to marry, so thankfully he couldn't join me just yet.

When I first went to Pakistan, there was a list of things I couldn't do because I didn't have a father. I was returning to the UK with the same lack of control, only now I belonged to a man who had power of veto over my life. My existence was once again defined by a man.

None of this was about me, about who I was or what I wanted. It was always about who I needed to be to satisfy the whims of another.

Once the first nikah was done, there was nothing to stop me from returning to Mum and my siblings. I couldn't believe I was finally leaving Pakistan. I had escaped, but I still didn't have my freedom. I had the chain of a nikah around my neck and I was returning as a married woman. I belonged to a man.

Once safely ensconced in the house, Mum took me aside.

'Why did you do it?' she demanded. 'Why did you marry Mazhar?'

I was immediately confused. 'Because you wanted me to!'

She burst into tears, shaking her head. But by then, it was too late.

And so, sometimes, this is how the dice fall, facilitated by miscommunication and interrupted long-distance phone calls and convoluted family emotional blackmail.

It was done. I was a married woman.

I was fifteen years old.

6

A Mattress for a Man

Once Mum realised that I hadn't wanted to marry Mazhar, that there had been a miscommunication between us with catastrophic results, her first idea was that I should get a divorce. I've already mentioned that Mum is both tough and determined when it comes to her kids, and if she felt that I had been wronged then she would support me all the way to a resolution. But the thing was, even though I was still a kid, I knew in my heart that I couldn't throw everything up in the air now.

Mum's marriage had failed: how would it look if I, too, had a broken marriage? For a start, Mum's izzat – low as it was – would never recover. My own status in the community and in the family: how would that fare? I asked myself what the benefit would be – for anyone – if I upset the apple cart now. Mum would suffer, Imy and Foz would suffer, I would suffer. And we would all become more isolated than ever. With my child's logic, I believed I just had to make it work.

It wasn't until I was in my thirties that I recognised that I had been groomed into marrying Mazhar. It had clearly been a forced marriage. Forced, because who chooses to get married to restore a family rift? Who tasks a fifteen-year-old with such a life-changing decision in the first place?

Once I was back in Bradford, there wasn't any mention of my continuing at school. I was a married woman now, waiting for my husband to join me. School was out of the question, despite my plans to get some qualifications.

Once again, I had no choice. I had to work to save money for Mazhar's ticket to the UK. I had a responsibility to do the right thing – the adult thing. And, despite the fact that the last thing I wanted was a husband, and because I've never been one to wallow, I just got on with it.

There were times when it struck me that my teenage years were missing something, probably the normal punctuation marks of adolescence – posters adorning the walls of a bedroom I didn't have to share, sleepovers with hushed gossip and midnight snacks. But there was no room for teenage angst in my life. Pushing through disappointment was a finely honed skill of mine by now, yet at the same time, I tried to believe Mum and my family in Pakistan were doing everything in my best interests.

I found a job working at the local nappy factory, where I spent my days stuffing defective premium brand nappies into boxes of fifty. The nappies had missing fasteners or slightly wonky seams and had failed quality standards tests, but there was still a market for them. They would be bought in bulk by factories whose workers (me) would fix them up to be sold on to local Asian stores in the area, who, in turn, would sell them to their customers. My first wage was £9 for a full week, which I gave to Mum as my contribution to the running the family home on Legrams Lane. From this sum, she would put a little aside for Mazhar's ticket.

Finally, I was able to shoulder a little of Mum's financial

burden. Aside from cigarettes and my daily copy of the *Sun*, I never went shopping for myself.

I worked at the nappy factory for most of 1989. In November, I turned sixteen and was sent back to Pakistan to complete my second nikah with Mazhar. I needed to do it again, because getting married at fifteen wasn't recognised in UK law for the purposes of applying for a visa. After a few months in Hamidabad Colony, where I shared quarters with Mazhar in another section of our horseshoe-shaped house, I returned to Bradford in early 1990 to start the process of Mazhar's visa application.

Well, you never know, I thought. I've heard of application cases taking years. I might be lucky.

I was a good girl who did what she was told, but in my heart, I hoped to never see him again.

After stuffing boxes with nappies, I moved on to washing the hospital linen at the Society of Linen Hire at an industrial warehouse in Usher Street. This was the main launderette for the NHS in Bradford, where I'd wash sheets and bedclothes all day long. I thought I'd really hit the big time when I moved on to packing crisps at the Seabrook crisps factory, where I was paid the handsome sum of £6 per hour – a whole £2 more than my last job. I did overtime whenever there was the opportunity, including cleaning the floors with an industrial buffer.

As part of this new adult life, I also discovered I liked dancing. Funnily enough, it was my dad who opened the door to this new world. That Christmas, the Seabrook Christmas party was taking place at a pub in Girlington, which was just around the corner from where my dad was living at the time. After my return from Pakistan, we had begun a tentative reconciliation, so I went round to see him one day after work.

'What are you doing out of work early?' he asked.

'They're having their Christmas party.'

'Well, why aren't you there?'

'It's in a pub. I can't go, can I?'

'Why not? You're not going to drink, are you?'

'Course not.'

'So why can't you go and have a dance with your mates? There's alcohol in Morrisons, isn't there, but no one says you can't go into Morrisons? You should go and enjoy yourself.'

Dad explained that provided I didn't drink or dress skimpily, and had no intention of flirting with men, it was fine by him. Maybe he remembered how I like to groove out to 'Brown Girl in the Ring' as a five-year-old and took pity on me.

Despite the disgrace he had brought into all our lives, my dad's word was still the law in our family – he had kept all his power. He was still our father, as my mother never failed to remind us.

He's been dead for over twenty years now, but if he were still alive, I have no doubt my mother would continue to insist we maintained a relationship with him. Even though I was a married woman, with my husband in Pakistan, I needed a man's blessing. Despite the pain he had caused my mum and my siblings, he was still my dad. When it concerned the Christmas party, as long as I obeyed the rules of izzat, Mum, too, was happy to concede.

Of course, if Mazhar had been there, there would have been no question of dancing at all. He was from a small village in

Pakistan, after all, raised within a culture where men were expected to uphold the patriarchy, and where women were utterly subservient to their husbands. But for the time being I had some freedom. From the Christmas party and beyond, I began to find a release in dancing.

It was desperate thinking, really, to hope that it might take years for Mazhar to get his visa. Wasn't it just my luck that his visa came through pretty much straight away? Within a couple of months, it was approved.

Mazhar arrived and we were legally married under UK law. I put up some pink wallpaper in the attic bedroom in Mum's house in Legrams Lane, with a double bed under the eaves. And there I was: a respectable married woman all of sixteen years old.

We weren't much of a married couple, just two kids who didn't know anything about each other apart from our shared experience of rural life in Pakistan.

We had consummated the marriage in Pakistan, when I went back for the second nikah. I had been absolutely petrified about the whole idea of sex, given I didn't know nearly enough to prepare myself; sex, like menstruation, was a taboo subject. If it wasn't bad enough that I was privately terrified of the wedding night, the whole episode had been so public.

After the ceremony, I was escorted by the community to Mazhar's quarters in the house in a ritual to welcome the new bride. My mother-in-law was adamant about seeing evidence of my virginity, also known as 'blood on the sheets'. And Mazhar informed me he would divorce me if I wasn't a virgin.

A MATTRESS FOR A MAN

It was all about duty – *my* duty to be precise. All evidence that I had ever had sex needed to be washed away when it was over. That's how it was in this rural community – sex was seen as a dirty habit.

I saw it as dirty, too, so thorough was my conditioning. There had been no concept of sexual pleasure. It was no surprise that I was scared. And honestly, the idea of a woman's pleasure was something that never crossed my mind.

Back in Bradford, after Mazhar had been living with us for a few months, Mum took me aside and told me that 'a woman has to be a mattress for a man'. Those were her exact words. According to Mum, a wife must make herself available to her husband whenever he desires sex. Chilling, I know.

I told her that wasn't going to work for me.

'In your day, Mum, maybe that was the case. But those days are over. I am not a mattress for a man.'

I felt so angry with her. At the time, it didn't occur to me to wonder why she might have drawn that conclusion.

Mazhar was the first adult man to live with us since my dad had left and even though Mum was the elder, and Mazhar respected her, there was an expectation that he would step into the role of man of the house. But as long as I still gave my wages to my mum and we all ate together every night, nothing much changed.

There was little affection between me and my new husband; we never held hands or cuddled up on the sofa to watch TV. We never shared details of our days or turned to each other in times of crisis. The lack of emotional intimacy meant that we were flatmates who shared a bed. But that's not quite true; flatmates tend to respect each other's space and desires.

Mazhar wasn't kind or thoughtful. He held me to a standard born of his own narrow belief system. I had to dress and behave in ways that suited his patriarchal notions of a 'good wife'. His suspicious nature required that I had to account for my whereabouts at all times.

Thankfully, I managed to avoid pregnancy, which was down to luck rather than planning. I had approached our local GP – a Muslim – before I went to Pakistan for the second nikah and asked him for the contraceptive pill. He refused, telling me that, 'If a soul is destined to be born, no amount of pills can stop it. You must put your faith in God.'

I did put my faith in God and, in my naivety, I prayed that all that washing after sex would flush away the possibility of a child with a man I was beginning to loathe.

Luckily, Mazhar was now working late shifts at a local restaurant and given that I worked all day, I didn't have to spend very much time with him at all.

During the few months I spent in Pakistan, Mazhar had shown just enough of his true nature to make me hope his visa application would be declined. He knew little of the Western culture within which I had been raised, and cared even less to find out. We had never exchanged love letters and, without evidence of affection, I assumed the immigration officer who interviewed me would turn him down and I could get on with my life. I had begun to think about my education again – that I might even go to university.

I was still working at Seabrook, Foz and Imy were at school, Mum was out all hours working at odd jobs. I needed to escape my husband's domineering attitudes and I wanted to escape a house that had become an unhappy home. I didn't know yet that Mum was being raped by Azam and his horrible mates – no matter the cost to her, she concealed her abuse from her three kids. We still thought of Uncle Azam as a kind, generous family friend, though we were intensely curious about the other men who kept calling.

Finally, in February 1992, after six months of living together, I'd had enough of Mazhar and his desire to control every aspect of my life. I had suspected how narrow-minded he was when once, in Pakistan at the time of our nikah, I had shaken hands with a male school friend and Mazhar had berated me. Men and women cannot be friends, he had insisted, it was inappropriate. Was this to be the rest of my life? A forensic scrutiny of my behaviour until I was reduced to a nodding, subjugated wife? While I might not have enjoyed the same freedoms as some of my school friends, I still had dreams and they would come to nothing if I stayed with this man.

The idea of leaving Mazhar had taken hold of me slowly. I felt suffocated in his presence, stifled in my attempts to find a little space for myself with friends or cousins. He was everywhere, setting the terms for my behaviour, my interactions with others, and I had begun to dread coming home from work to find him waiting for me. It became obvious to me that our situation, in the long term, was unendurable. I told Mum that I had had enough, that I wanted to go back to school and that I would have no chance at an education if I stayed married to Mazhar.

I decided to save enough money for a few months' rent, food and bills. When the time was right, I would hand in my notice at work and leave. Once I was settled elsewhere, I would enrol in some college courses.

When I could stand Mazhar no longer, I quit work and moved to Watford to stay with a friend.

I was by no means the first woman in my community to run away. There were plenty of stories of girls who had fled restrictive upbringings to live their own lives.

I didn't believe I would never see Mum or my siblings again – my intention was to make a good life for myself and return one day. In the back of my mind was the lingering fear that Foz would be subject to the same sort of forced marriage that I had endured. The idea of Foz marrying Mazhar's younger brother had been mooted in the past and I was crystal clear that I would move heaven and hell to stop that from happening.

There were no mobile phones in those days, and I hadn't left a single clue as to my whereabouts. After a few weeks of camping out in the house my friend shared with some other students, I rang Mum, who told me that I had caused a huge ruckus in the community – everyone was asking where I'd gone and who I might be with. She was crying, pleading with me to come home. Given that Mazhar was her nephew, she considered it a shame upon the family that I'd left him. When I told her I wouldn't come home if Mazhar remained in the house, she lied to me. She assured me that her family had sent him to Germany to find work there, now that his marriage was over. And so, reluctantly – ever the obedient daughter – I returned. I had agreed to the marriage out of obligation to my mum and she had sent Mazhar away for me, so now it was only right that I went back.

I returned to discover that Mazhar was not in Germany. He was staying at his cousin's house in Bradford. But before I could make any more decisions about the direction of my life, my whole world turned upside down.

7

On Remand

On 11 April 1992, Azam died as a result of complications from gastroenteritis.

He was always kind and generous towards me, and his death was a terrible shock. Whenever I came home to Legrams Lane after work, Uncle Azam's regular presence in the house was a comfort, particularly after Mazhar moved in. Of medium build, with distinctive pockmarks across his face from smallpox, he represented an older, reliable male figure in the absence of my own dad.

Even though he lived with his wife and family a couple of miles away, he was such a regular fixture that I came to rely on his presence for some proper, old-school masculine benevolence. He was the family friend who had helped Mum to buy the house in the first place, and yes, while he might have had his own stint in prison, he was still an important source of stability for me.

Although he was married and we knew his family, without ever asking about it or being told about it, I knew that there was 'something' going on between Azam and my mum. To me, Azam was a nice man, so much so that I had relaxed my opinion about Mum having a boyfriend. I could turn a blind eye while still maintaining my private belief that their 'relationship' was dishonourable – he was a married man, after all, and there's no 'dating' or 'boyfriends' in my culture. I hadn't been raised to ask questions, so there was no way I would have ever challenged Mum on what she was doing.

But that's all I knew. I had no idea of the horrific reality that lay behind that 'something'.

Everything changed with Azam's sudden and unexpected death. For the first few days, I couldn't quite process what had happened. I didn't think twice when, without warning, Mum sent my little sister Foz, who was just eleven years old, to Pakistan to spend time in Hamidabad Colony with our family. Foz was happy enough to go – Pakistan was a home away from home for her. We thought she'd be away for a couple of weeks, a month at most.

I thought back to when I was twelve and packed off to Pakistan. Would Foz be away for two and a half years and return a married woman? I was too consumed with grief for Azam to think much about it.

Before long, strange rumours and stories began to circulate within the community about Azam, about Mum, and about how the relationship between the two of them was much more complex than I had imagined. I had no idea, and wouldn't know for years, that in fact Mum was in a coercive, abusive relationship with him. Much more shocking were the terrible rumours swirling that Azam had in some way behaved badly towards me – and that Mum had killed him.

These were dark days. Once again, we were the subjects of gossip and innuendo. I wanted to mourn Azam – I was so upset by his death. I didn't want my head filled with this toxic gossip and I was extremely offended by the suggestion that Azam had ever abused me. Being shunned by the community was bad enough, but being the talk of the town was worse. There was, as usual, no sign of my dad. We were on our own again, treading water.

In accordance with Muslim practice, Azam was buried the day after his death and his family and the community mourned. But Azam's wife had shared some concerns with the coroner's office; she believed that Azam had been poisoned and had kept a sample of his vomit to be tested. A few days later, the results came back from the coroner's office, confirming that arsenic was present in the sample. Shortly after, the police arrived at Legrams Lane, asking who had cooked the meal we had shared with Azam on the night of his death. When I told them that I had prepared the curry and Mum had made the samosas and Azam's dessert, we were both arrested on suspicion of murder.

Nothing could have prepared me or Mum for what followed. To be accused of such a serious crime when I knew, without a shadow of a doubt, that we were innocent, that I could never have dreamt of committing such an act, was horrific.

At the same time, the accusation seemed so crazy to me, so laughable, that I was quite light-hearted with the officers down at the police station. The clothes I was wearing were taken away and I was given a white, lightweight offender's outfit to wear instead. I remember joking with the policemen about how foxy I must look in that get-up. They were just as playful with me, calling me 'petal' and even giving me magazines to read. It all seemed like a strange dream, a mad mistake that I'd be able to laugh about with my friends once the police realised it was all nonsense.

I didn't know at the time that their levity was calculated. Murder is a serious offence to be charged with, and with that comes the risk of suicide – that's why they were being so nice. I had interpreted their care as a tacit acknowledgement that a grave mistake had been made. Put simply, I saw the whole episode as a fuck-up on the part of the police. As far as I was concerned, my beloved uncle had just died, my siblings and I were grieving, and the police were wasting their time with this rubbish.

I was still pretty naive back then, even at the age of eighteen. I hadn't had a happy childhood or adolescence and I hadn't achieved the traditional milestones that my peers had. My experiences were so alien compared to those of my community – my father had brought untold shame onto our family, I had spent years moving around Bradford, and at fifteen I had been married off to my cousin. My achievements were running a farm and cooking and cleaning for my family in Pakistan. Those were my landmarks, my milestones – not GCSEs, best friends or fashion. I was defined as a successful person by the chores I could complete, by how willing a mattress I could be. The only thing I had ever wanted for myself was to have a fringe at the age of twelve.

The next day, Mum and I were released pending investigations.

That's when the reality of our situation struck; we were on the front page of the local newspapers: *Mother and daughter arrested on suspicion of murdering local man.* The community rumour mill went into overdrive. Once again, the Shah name was on everyone's lips. More rumours emerged about Mum, about Azam, and about Mum and other men. I felt completely overwhelmed. All the pain and hurt of the last two years with Mazhar, the breakup of my family, and now these stories of murder and abuse combined to make everything seem hopeless. I just couldn't see any way forward.

Raised with the absolute conviction that the British justice system was the best in the world, that mistakes were very rarely made and that the law was on the side of the good, I felt baffled and betrayed by the police. It was the consensus of our relatives in Pakistan that we were privileged to live in Britain. A photo of the Queen held pride of place in our sitting room; we were very grateful to the UK and heartily agreed we were living in the best country in the world. It was obvious this was a catastrophic miscarriage of justice and that very soon, it would be corrected.

But the chaos of our lives was overwhelming. In a moment of desperation, I went to the bathroom cupboard and found a couple of boxes of Diclofenac painkillers, scooped all the pills into my hand and guzzled them down with a glass of water.

I'd had enough. I was out of here.

I wasn't thinking about anyone else in that moment, not my mother or my siblings. The rumours, the arrests, the mayhem – I couldn't see another way out. You might think my faith would have offered me some guidance at this point, but God didn't come into the equation. If my faith had been stronger or if I'd understood it the way I do today, I would have trusted God. I would have trusted that these trials were sent to us by God, that God tests those He loves. But I was raised to fear God, not love Him. Heaven and hell were our daily lessons. Punishment served by hell was for the wicked; heaven awaited those who lived devout lives. My cultural understanding of Islam didn't extend beyond the missive to keep God happy and not risk His wrath. It wouldn't have crossed my mind to thank God and turn to Him during the nightmare we found ourselves in.

These days, I turn to God and thank him for every experience and accept that He is in charge and that I don't control anything. While I might not like challenging situations – while I might not enjoy feeling angry or vulnerable – today, I accept these burdens. I accept that God has a better plan for me.

Looking back, both these separate but interlinked events – my being accused of murder, my attempt at suicide – clearly demonstrate to me just how perilous anyone's life can be if the foundations upon which that life is built are shaken by outside events. We like to think that we are all quite capable of dealing with life's blows, but a safe and secure existence in which we're surrounded by family and friends and colleagues can very swiftly crumble, given the right circumstances. It seems extraordinary that someone could seriously consider taking their life – in many ways, it seems even more extraordinary now that that someone was me – but what I've processed from my experience is that we always need to be vigilant when considering those within our own circles who may need extra support.

Mental health crises can strike anyone at any time, often arising unexpectedly and involving those you might never previously have suspected of such vulnerability. More and more, I think it is one of our citizen duties to be watchful for the signs.

Despite the attempt, it turned out I wasn't out of here. I ended up in hospital having my stomach pumped with activated charcoal, a particularly horrible but lifesaving procedure. At that moment, with capable and caring nurses standing over my bed, I felt utterly adrift and alone. Mum was distraught. *How could you do this?* she asked me over and over. *How could you think of leaving us?* I know she was hurt, scared and bewildered, but it felt like I was being reprimanded.

I was sent home from the hospital (my poo was black for weeks afterwards from the charcoal), and now it was like we were living in our very own siege movie.

I was shaken, confused and unhappy. But, as usual, I got on with the business of life. I promised Mum I wouldn't do it again and, as usual, we didn't dig any deeper, never delving into the whys.

The Shah name was on the front pages of the papers every day, only now it was national press and TV, including on the *News at Ten*. People stared at us in the street if we ever ventured out. No one from the family contacted us – if Mum made phone calls, they went unanswered. There were endless police visits and interviews at the station. There were more rumours than we could process. But everything seemed utterly incomprehensible to me – of course Mum hadn't killed Azam. Why wouldn't everyone just pull themselves together and realise that this was a crazy mistake? What was wrong with them? Hadn't my mum suffered enough in her life already?

Mum and I never once talked about the rumours, about the accusations, or about the details of her relationship with

Azam. We didn't have a modern parent–child relationship – it may be hard to imagine today, but certain subjects were off the table, including my reasons for attempting suicide.

Mum and I were arrested again and then released again.

The only blessing as those terrible weeks swirled by was that little Foz was protected from the unfolding catastrophe. I'm thankful that she didn't have to suffer that torment, but looking back, I feel terrible about the impact on my poor fourteen-year-old brother, Imy. Our lives were so bewildering I didn't even have time to worry about how this might be affecting him. Imy withdrew into himself; he was clearly being neglected, and at a loss as to what on earth was going on in our family. For the first time, I was glad Foz wasn't there to see it; she was one less person to worry about.

Once I realised I probably shouldn't have attempted suicide, that it was no way to deal with the nightmare we had been catapulted into, I told myself we were survivors, we Shahs. We'd get through this madness, life would get back to normal and then we'd all be OK again.

Mum's constant reassurances that everything would sort itself out did little to stem the rising chaos of this period and we waded through these days taking each as it came. That was how it went until 27 July, when we were hit with what felt like a bolt of thunder.

The third time the police came to our house, Mum alone was arrested. It was made clear to me that I was no longer under any suspicion. The forensics had revealed arsenic in the *gajrela*, a sweet dessert made of carrots that Mum had prepared for Azam only. It was confirmed that there was no arsenic in the curry I had cooked. I had supplied fingernail scrapings and strands of hair, and the results showed that I, too, had ingested some traces of arsenic but probably as cross contamination from the dessert.

Mum was formally charged with the murder of Azam. She was taken away and sent on remand to New Hall Prison near Wakefield.

Imy and I were on our own.

The next few months went by in a blur.

It was my absolute conviction that Mum was innocent and that her place was back at home looking after her children. I never for one second swerved from that certainty. An injustice had been committed; prison was no place for our mother, and a desperate urgency to get her out was to become my sole focus.

I'll never forget the first time I went to visit her when she was on remand in New Hall Prison. I went on my own so that I could get the lay of the land before I took Imy with me. It was a scary, alien place on the outskirts of Wakefield, filled with clanging doors, metal tables and staccato voices issuing orders.

When I arrived at the visitor's hall, Mum looked tinier than ever. She seemed to have shrunk into herself in this strange new environment. And when I rose to leave at the end of that visit, her dark eyes widened with fear and a terrible desperation. It was like the first time you take your child to nursery school – you don't want to leave them and they don't want you to go. That look beamed a message into my soul: pleading and pathetic, she was saying, *Naz, don't leave me here. Please.* That was the day our roles were irrevocably reversed. I became the mother, and she the child. Just like a three-year-old learning to survive in an alien environment without their parent, my mother had to find a way to navigate life in prison.

This parental role had been foisted upon me. I had no say in this matter – just like I'd had no say in any of the decisions made about my life. I wasn't ready to step into Mum's shoes, but these were the cards we had been dealt and I had to keep moving forward.

I visited Mum with Imy five days a week – a six-hour round trip from home to the prison and back again. I didn't have the time to process how Imy was dealing with the situation beyond my reassurances that it would all be fine, that Mum would soon be released, that Foz would return and we would be a family once more. For the first time in my life, I signed on for various social security benefits, but I struggled to budget our household finances. The money would often be swallowed up within days of receiving it. The cost of travelling to and from prison was substantial. We also supplied Mum with phone cards so she could stay in touch with us and her relatives in Pakistan. Then there were the tea and biscuits we bought to share with her on our visits, and on top of that, we gave her spending money. Imy and I survived on Pot Noodles and dahl, despite the fact I had started to pawn whatever jewellery I owned, convincing myself that I didn't care for gold anyway. It wasn't until I was in my forties that I would start to wear it again.

Each morning, before we left for the prison, I would run round to the offices of the solicitors who were handling Mum's case to make sure I was up to date on its progress. There were old stories being dragged out, including the time when Mum had, apparently, paid a local taxi driver in gold bangles to murder Azam. According to this particular rumour, Mum decided she wanted to kill Azam in 1990 because he wouldn't sign over the house she rightfully believed was hers; the taxi driver told Azam about Mum's plans and Azam went to the police. The courts decided that tale was too far-fetched to take seriously, and Mum was bound over to keep the peace. (The irony here is that, had Mum taken some legal advice, she might have been determined to be the beneficial owner of the house anyway, given that she had made all the mortgage payments.)

What did these people think was going on? Our lives weren't an episode of *The Sopranos*. This was my mum, Zoora Shah, a poor innocent woman who had worked her fingers to the bone to bring up her kids after being cast aside by her own community. I had to do everything I could to rescue her from the appalling treatment she was suffering. I knew she was innocent and so would the courts once we had assembled all the information. I was determined that she would come back home to us.

In Pakistan, the family was in a spin. Mum's dishonour cast a long shadow and the shame she laid at the feet of her relatives was almost unfathomable. Those that didn't believe the gossip visited holy shrines and prayed for the truth to come out – like me, they were convinced she had been framed and that a big mistake had been made. *Pirs*, holy men, were engaged to try to lift the spell that had been cast on Mum's integrity, as it was assumed a jinn had put arsenic in Azam's food.

Things began to unravel at home, too. While Foz was being cared for in Pakistan, my brother was struggling. My reassurances that everything would eventually be OK did little to comfort him. Between meetings with the solicitors and the daily trek to New Hall, I just didn't have the time – or the skills – to help him process his feelings about the disaster that had befallen our lives. Poor Imy had to deal with so much of it on his own. He started skipping school and smoking cigarettes.

There were no responsible adults around to help us navigate this new territory. All I had to guide me were my cultural norms: that alcohol was forbidden, that dressing modestly was paramount and that boyfriends were out of the question. But how could these rules help me raise and comfort a young boy?

After I had been verbally abused in the butcher's – a neighbour shouted, 'There goes the daughter of a murderer', while others around her nodded their heads in agreement – Imy and I stopped venturing out into the community.

Isolated and frustrated, things would occasionally blow up between me and my brother. He once dumped a whole plate of spaghetti Bolognese on my head. He had a thing about throwing food, I guess, because not long after, he hurled his pizza into the air, leaving a patchwork of mozzarella and tomato sauce on the ceiling. We rarely argued about the impact Mum's arrest was having on our lives. Instead, we bickered about small, insignificant things – that there was no salt in the house, no hot water or no clean pants. This was the way we expressed our heartbreak.

To defer my rising panic, I reassured myself that once Mum was free she would deal with Imy and bring Foz home.

We sorely needed some outside intervention, but none was

forthcoming from social services or any other organisation. For the few remaining community members who still talked to us, Mum's incarceration was the final straw. Horrified by the scandal, they turned their backs on us once and for all. Poor Imy was pretty much left to deal with the trauma on his own; how could I blame him for hiding his pain by playing up? Of course, I wish I had been a wiser sister, more considerate of his feelings, but life is never so simple. Besides, I had additional problems of my own.

Once again, Dad made a tentative re-entry into our lives. He soon began to put pressure on me to reunite with Mazhar. In no uncertain terms, he told me that it wasn't 'appropriate' for a twenty-year-old married woman to be living alone. Mazhar had to return to Legrams Lane and the marriage for the sake of our izzat – with Mum all over the front pages of the tabloids, our honour was in shreds.

It may come as some surprise to learn that I capitulated. The pressure from the family was enormous. I was a girl without her mother; I had no security at all anymore and now our shame had reached monumental levels, I was desperate enough to do anything that would make me feel better. The idea of returning to my husband was better than having nobody and no izzat. And for *some* izzat, I'd need a man in the house. I badly wanted someone to share my pain, to tell me everything would be all right, but Mazhar and I didn't have that sort of relationship. While he filled the husband-shaped space as mandated by izzat, he was anything but a friend. Deep down, I knew it was the wrong thing to do. But despair had driven me to consider the unimaginable.

*

Mum's case finally came to be heard at the Crown Court in Leeds in November 1993. It would take four weeks and I attended every session. Each morning, when I left for court, I told Imy that it wouldn't be long before the trial was over and Mum would be back home with us. I was still convinced that she was innocent. Our solicitor, Stephen Murdoch of TI Clough & Co Solicitors in Bradford, was a big, bearded guy who looked a bit like the actor Brian Blessed. He had a larger-than-life personality and a way with words, which was why he was good at what he did. Over the months, he'd never said or done anything that led me to question Mum's innocence.

Should he or others have done more to manage my expectations? Maybe. But perhaps people wanted to protect me from the possibility that my mum might have taken a man's life. Not for one moment did I believe that Mum had killed Azam. Not for a single second. It was the gastroenteritis that had killed him.

In court, Mum was standing trial accused of four crimes, to which she pleaded not guilty. She was accused of attempting to forge mortgage and land registry papers so that Azam's name would be removed from ownership of Legrams Lane, of soliciting another person to murder him, of attempted murder and, finally, she was accused of murder.

Two of these accusations weren't a surprise to me or my siblings. We knew about the local taxi driver Mum had tried to hire to kill Azam. It was an absurd situation and the idea of Mum approaching a local guy and offering him a few pieces of her jewellery to kill another man displays the level of such an amateur attempt. The document forgery was an equally cack-handed attempt to get the house signed over into her name, her justification being that she had paid the deposit and all the mortgage payments. Despite these incidents, I didn't believe for a second that Mum could have poisoned someone. I didn't believe she was capable of murder. And if she was going to kill Azam, she wouldn't have risked the lives of two of her children who, it was proved, had traces of arsenic in their blood. What stupid woman would risk poisoning her own offspring? There was no way that I could believe Mum had not only murdered someone but risked our lives into the bargain.

Every day, she and I looked at each other across that courtroom. Her eyes locked onto mine as though holding on to a life raft. *Don't leave me,* those eyes said. *Don't leave me.* Imy never came to the trial, he was at school, but I would fill him in every evening.

The prosecution depicted Mum as a cunning, manipulative criminal. They claimed she had inserted arsenic into the *gajrela* – the dessert – which she had given Azam the night before he died. The police had also found traces of arsenic in the forensics they'd taken from me when I was first arrested: it appeared there was also arsenic in the samosas that Imy and I had eaten the same night, but not in sufficient quantity to hurt us. They painted her as a terrible mother for endangering the lives of her own children, but we knew Mum loved us unconditionally and the idea that she might put us at risk was impossible to consider. It's impossible to consider even now.

The papers reported, daily, the explosive details as they were revealed. To prove that Azam had died from arsenic poisoning, his body had had to be exhumed from its grave soon after he'd been buried. It was the first case of an exhumation in a criminal case in almost a hundred years. Wild media speculation accompanied the daily court reports. Mum was painted as an avaricious person who had attempted fraud in order to make herself the legal owner of a property that belonged to Azam. There was nothing to which this woman wouldn't stoop in order to further her aims.

And this terrible woman – this supposed demon – sat across the way from me every day in that courtroom with terror in her eyes.

I gazed back at her, oblivious to the true depths of the suffering she had endured all those years. Despite everything she had experienced ever since she'd first left Pakistan to come to England to marry my dad, despite finding herself in court accused of such a horrific crime, she clung to her izzat. She refused to shame herself or her children by telling anyone what had been done to her.

She kept her mouth shut because of what she understood to be honour – the honour of her family – despite the fact it had been snatched away from her time and again. She wouldn't reveal the truth of her life, because she didn't want to make things any worse for her children than they already were. But also, as I see it now, I think Mum didn't talk because she was at the end of her tether. She was hollowed out by the gruelling life she had been forced to endure all these years. She was exhausted by the violence, the shunning by her community and family, the poverty, the abuse. And her refusal to engage makes a sick sort of sense, too. After everything she'd gone through – after suffering in silence for all those years – she no longer believed there was any hope for her at all. She believed that the outcome of the trial had already been decided, and that nothing she could say would make the slightest difference.

Finally, it was the day of the verdict. One of the women I'd met visiting Mum in New Hall, who'd clearly had experience of the criminal world and the ways in which the courts operated, had told me that when the verdict is reached in any trial, you could bet your bottom dollar that if the jury looked at the accused, that would mean a 'not guilty' verdict. So, after deliberating, as each of the jurors filed back into the courtroom that day, I was watching their eyes as they took their seats. My heart sank a little with every juror. None of them looked at Mum. Not even the foreman of the jury. He just stared straight ahead at the judge.

My heart fell into my stomach.

The judge asked the foreman whether they had reached a verdict.

'Yes,' he replied. My very last hope was shattered into pieces, pieces which to this day have never fully come back together.

The judge read out all four counts and the foreman gave the jury's verdict.

'Forgery.'

'Guilty.'

'Soliciting murder.'

'Guilty.'

'Attempted murder.'

'Guilty.'

'Murder.'

'Guilty.'

And there it was. Mum wasn't coming home.

ON REMAND

We were in one of the larger courtrooms in Leeds Crown Court, the jury across the room, the judge perched on his bench. At the back of the courtroom sat my mum, her eyes still on mine as the verdict was read out. The rest of the room was a blur; at that moment it was just me and her. It felt like one of those slow-motion moments in a movie where the room spins around, but you remain stock-still. It was like being in the centre of a storm. A tornado of voices poured forth, screaming, shouting from every corner. My head was spinning. Adrenaline, anger and shock surged through me. How could they think she was guilty?

I'm staring at Mum and her eyes are begging me not to cry. They're hugging me and trying to protect me from afar but never quite reaching me. I can see she's desperately trying to soothe my pain as any mother would, but she can't, she's too far away. Her left hand is clasping the rail in front of her and her right hand is held up to her mouth, trying to stop herself from crying. But it's no use – she's breaking down and I'm breaking down.

I'll never forget that look of utter fear, defeat and helplessness on my mum's face. She wasn't coming home.

The day that Mum was found guilty I believed I'd witnessed a monumental miscarriage of justice. It was a mistake, and I would fix it. I had no idea how, but I knew I would. Not in my wildest dreams did I understand the implications – the severity – of what that 'guilty of murder' verdict really meant.

But as I stood there in shock, watching my mother diminish in front of my eyes, I believed this was the most disastrous thing that ever happened to me and my family. During the course of the next few years I was to learn otherwise.

The nightmare had only just begun.

8

Sofa Surfer

My teenage years came to an end in that courtroom.

At the start of the trial, in November 1993, I turned twenty – the same number the judge came up with when he pronounced his sentencing on Mum the following month. Life, or a minimum tariff of twenty years. I would be forty before I would see my mum outside of a prison again. It was a blow so shattering, such a magnificent miscarriage of justice, that I couldn't really take it in. It was like the beginning of a nightmare I knew I would never wake from.

From today's vantage point, it would be fair to say that this period was to define my future in politics. Before long, the trauma of the previous eighteen months and the finality of the judgment would be replaced by a fierce rage. It is a rage that continues to fuel my commitment to challenge sheer bloody injustice when I see it. Over the next couple of decades – before I finally became an elected politician – I would learn how to channel that fury into practical campaigning and leadership skills, working to prevent others from feeling they have no other path to follow than the most dangerous: one that offers little hope and an almost certain downfall. I may give the appearance of calm competence – which is how I must present myself in order to meet my obligations to my constituents every day – but beneath the surface, my politics are stoked by a powerful fire. That fire can be distilled into a very simple code: it's unacceptable for any man, woman or child to have to experience inequality, discrimination or abuse of any kind in any culture or country across the world. Full stop.

I should say that while I may be driven by rage, I am not driven blindly and not without a destination. My passion, shaped by learning and experience, informs a view of politics that reaches beyond the usual party political mantras. Today's media – especially social media – tries to drive wedges between political leaders based on soundbites and scandal, when really we should be linking arms across the divide to find solutions together for the people we represent. After all, isn't that what our constituents have voted for? Someone to champion their interests?

These would be thoughts for the future, however. On the morning of 21 December 1993, as Mum was led away from the courtroom, I had something else on my mind. My brother, Imy.

I took a deep breath and pushed open the front door of our house. Imy was in the hallway, still in his *taqiyah* (the skullcap he wears to the mosque) and clutching a handful of dried kidney beans and date seeds. Every Muslim house in Bradford had a stash of these, used as counters for prayers.

Imy's eyes were wide with excitement and anticipation. But very quickly he understood that the previous night we'd spent praying that Mum would be found innocent and freed was wasted.

I could feel my eyes welling up, my guts churning. It's that feeling in the pit of your stomach when your teacher tells you off in primary school and you want to cry but you're trying your hardest not to in front of the whole class. The tears tend to come anyway. The difference was that I wasn't at school, and I wasn't a child any more. I was an adult woman, standing before my fifteen-year-old brother, to whom I'd promised to bring our mother back.

How I even took those few steps to hold him in my arms, I don't know. But somehow I did. We hugged and cried and cried. I didn't need to tell Imy the verdict – he understood that Mum wouldn't be back any time soon. It was a helpless, hopeless feeling, and another blow in a life beset by them.

We'd never really celebrated Christmas in a big way – just a small tree placed in the bay window, adorned with red-striped candy canes and bits of holly hung just so. But there was to be no festive cheer that year for me and Imy.

Foz was still in Pakistan and had no idea what was going on, whereas Imy had lived every painful second of the last few months with me: the arrests, the bail applications, the solicitors, the trial, the terrible publicity.

He had once been a model student and model son. The good-looking kid that every mother would want. He had an infectious personality and was so laid-back that if you flicked him, he'd fall over. A happy-go-lucky, positive kid. But that had all changed. He had gone from model student to truant. And who could blame him? His world turned upside down, Imy was at a loss to make sense of everything that had happened to us.

Imy and I didn't know how to talk to each other. We had

never shared our feelings about anything significant in the past – Mum wasn't one to sit down for a heart-to-heart. It wasn't part of our familial vocabulary. But she would have known how to manage Imy then, how to soothe and comfort him, how to set him back on the right track.

I, on the other hand, had no idea.

While we were poor, Mum had a keen eye for a bargain and was a saver. Heavily discounted clothes from ex-catalogues furnished our wardrobes, and because he was a boy and her only son, Imy was – by our standards – a little spoilt. When I started working, we had a bit more money, which meant Imy lucked out: he'd always been the best-dressed kid in school. He had a BMX bike and a Sega computer console. He was the popular one among his friends and in the neighbourhood. His skinny frame had earnt him the nickname 'Boney', and his dress sense had earnt him a secondary name, 'Stud'.

Until Mazhar joined the household, Imy enjoyed his status as the only man in the household. But the golden boy was now suffering so much, my heart ached for him. I sold one of my few remaining pieces of gold jewellery just so I could buy him the computer game he wanted, in the hope it would give him a little pleasure. I was trying hard to be both mum and big sister – an impossible hybrid role I just couldn't seem to manage. While I urged him to go to school, I didn't follow through with his teachers, where I might have discussed Imy's needs in detail. I never attended a parents' evening. Given I was little more than a child myself, I hadn't had enough life experience to navigate the path we were on. Our lives were in chaos, and for much of the time I was just waiting for the next thing to go wrong.

With no support from family or community, we had effectively been cast out. Without honour or izzat, we had no one to turn to. But instinctively I knew I had to hold the family together. I had to hold my brother close.

Today, there is a more integrated approach to situations like the one we faced, with systems such as the Women's Prison Project stepping in when mothers are imprisoned to ensure that children are cared for in her absence. But back in 1993, we had none of that support – we weren't even on any social services register. There was one very kindly Anglican vicar who attended the court hearings and who came to see me afterwards to ask if I needed help, but he was the only person who reached out to us during those dark days.

If we were going to survive, we would need to hold on to each other and that meant we needed to get our sister back; we had to hang on to the family we had in the absence of family who wanted no part of our lives. I didn't know how much Foz was aware of at this point. Communications with the little hamlet of Hamidabad Colony were so limited, and we all felt she was better off being away from the media intrusion, police visits and courtroom drama. But while she'd been safer with our relatives in Pakistan, it was now time to bring her home. I used the last of my savings to buy a ticket to Pakistan for Imy, telling him I was sending him over to bring our sister back. He, too, was desperate to have Foz home again. With just two years between them, they were closer to each other than they were to me and they missed each other deeply. Sure, he would have to stay put until I managed to save enough money to fly them both back, but I held on to the idea that we would all be together again soon.

Imy left soon after Christmas and I was all that was left of our family.

After Mum's conviction, she had been relocated from New Hall in Wakefield to Durham Prison, a good hundred miles away up north. Mazhar and I decided to rent out Legrams Lane and we moved into a house in Heidelberg Road. We couldn't live in the family home any longer – it had too many negative associations and we couldn't bear the sidelong looks of our neighbours.

I felt utterly lost and very much alone. I couldn't make sense of the fact that my world had narrowed down to this unimaginable destiny – my mother in prison, my siblings so far away.

Missing my mum and my siblings, the only thing I could think to do was pray. For the first time in my life, I practised *i'tikaf* – one of the meditative traditions of my religion which is practised during the last ten days of Ramadan, and the faithful equivalent of half of a pilgrimage to Mecca. For those ten days, I secluded myself from the world behind a curtain at my cousin's house, praying all day, speaking to no one, attempting to get closer to God – hoping that when I emerged I would have a better understanding of what was happening to me. I even forewent my visits to Mum during this period, believing that I had to sacrifice something so precious to me to prove to God that I was sincere in my devotion to Him. After ten days of prayer and contemplation, the hope is that you will emerge with your faith reinforced and your commitment to worship stronger than ever. Cleansing and beneficial, i'tikaf allows you to focus your mind on your belief and in the healing power of God.

Even though I sat i'tikaf, I wouldn't say it was the dawning of my faith as I understand it today – that came later. I observed my *namaz* – my prayers – but I didn't understand a word of what I was reading. I viewed this period of retreat as a transactional exchange: all I wanted was for Mum to be released from prison, so that's what I prayed for. I would sit in prayer and contemplation, put my life on hold for ten days, and at the end of it, God would heed my call. While I hoped for a spiritual release, the truth is, I was wishing for a miracle.

However, I emerged from i'tikaf certain about one thing: it was time to leave Mazhar for good.

Had my faith been stronger at the time, I would never have taken Mazhar back in the first place – despite my father's insistence that I needed a man in the house. While, as Muslims, it is our duty to look after our precious bodies – a gift from God – and our mental health, a large part of my community had a patriarchal cultural understanding of our faith, rather than an Islamic one, and turning a blind eye to abuse, whether verbal, emotional or physical, was a cultural norm. No one would help me; I had to get out of this mess myself.

Yet I must also acknowledge that the cultural pressure to maintain our izzat and to return my mother's izzat to her kept me and my siblings together and drove us to fight for justice for Mum.

My mother, who would give her last morsel of food to someone in need, had been imprisoned for a crime she didn't commit. Her children were living apart and still so young.

Her ex-husband cared nothing for her or his kids. You might ask, where was God's benevolence in all this chaos? It's a good question. But it's the wrong question. In my faith, we see catastrophe as a test, not a calamity, and God only tests those He loves. The more trials and tribulations we suffer in life, the more we turn to God. At this point in my life, I couldn't honestly claim to have plumbed the spiritual depths of my religion – that was to come later – but my faith was deeply embedded nonetheless. All I knew was that the bad luck that had befallen us was out of my hands. It was out of the hands of all mortals. I had to turn to God.

After I had finished i'tikaf, I left my cousin's house and went back to Heidelberg Road, to the house I was sharing with Mazhar. His jacket lay over a chair in the kitchen, and I noticed a letter sticking out of a pocket. That night, while he slept, I opened the letter and read. It was obvious he was in some sort of relationship with the author of this note.

The single strangest thing about this episode was that it was Mazhar's emotional infidelity that finally sanctioned my separation from my husband. It wasn't the controlling behaviour, his lack of affection or the contempt in his voice when he spoke to me. It wasn't his suspicious nature or his dogged refusal to look beyond his narrow-minded upbringing. It was an affair of the heart. His treatment of me was acceptable in my community, but I didn't have to accept it if he was cheating.

I'd laugh if it wasn't so pathetic.

When I confronted Mazhar, he denied any affair and ridiculed me for even suggesting it. Gaslighting much? I packed up a few clothes and left the house for my cousin's. But that wasn't the end of it. Mazhar was intent on getting me back. He came to my workplace – I was now working at a mortgage company as an administrative assistant – and verbally abused me, accusing me of having an affair with my boss.

Again and again, I told him it was over and that I was going to seek a divorce. One way or another, we were done.

From today's vantage point, I believe that God heard and helped me during i'tikaf. Even though I was asking for something else entirely, part of my burden – Mazhar – had been lifted in anticipation of the fight that lay ahead. The fight for Mum.

During this period, even when I felt my stress so acutely, I still didn't turn to prayer. I hadn't grown up watching my mum pray, and despite my ten days of contemplation, I hadn't yet acquired the habit myself. I'm not even sure we had a Qur'an in the house.

Instead of praying, I turned to dancing. It was exactly the sort of outlet I needed to help me shake away – just for a few hours – what I was going through.

Tuesday nights were ladies' nights at the Park pub and I'd go into town and dance the night away. We also went down to the Boiler House and the Courthouse on Thursday, Friday and Saturday nights, and finished the week on Sunday with the Old Cornmill, downing cans of Red Bull to give me extra energy to burn. I had a pair of black trousers that I had to adjust with a safety pin because I was so skinny. I'd always be first on the dancefloor and the last to leave. I'd dance for eight hours at a stretch. I was as fit as a butcher's dog.

I'd met my regular dancing buddies, Niki and Sheridan,

while out clubbing. We were a trio of groovers and thick as thieves. I only wanted to dance, rejecting the drinks offered to me and the boys who wanted to chat me up. I was the best, and cheapest, friend to go out dancing with, because I was – and still am – teetotal and could also be relied upon to take anyone who had enjoyed a beer or two to their doorstep at the end of the night.

Bhangra, R&B, hip-hop, soul, Tony Braxton, Jagged Edge, Black Street – I loved it all. Dancing was – still is, occasionally – a way of shutting out some of the pain of my everyday life. I could drown in the sound.

But dancing couldn't keep the real world at bay forever.

My cousin had her own family to think about and within a few weeks it was time to move on. I suddenly found myself alone and homeless.

When I walk down the streets of any sizable city these days and see people sleeping in the doorways of empty shops, I wonder about their last experience of home. What happened to set them adrift? It's an easy, precipitous fall to take. One day, you have a key to a room where you have a bed; the next, you're standing in the street, wondering what to do and where you might grab a few hours' sleep.

There are many paths to homelessness – mental health issues, family arguments, social isolation and loss of employment, to name just a few. Without a strong support network in times of distress, it's too easy to move from home to homelessness, in full view of the world.

I had been trying to escape my husband for such a long time that I had no doubts about finally closing the door on our marriage. But then I found that I, too, had no support network. Just twenty years old, I had little money and no qualifications. Neither my family nor my community wanted to know me, the killer's daughter, never mind extend the hand of charity or mercy. Having had my face plastered all over the front pages of the national press crushed any desire in me to head down to the local employment office. Taunts and accusatory stares dogged my footsteps. If my siblings were to come home, I had to buy their tickets and to do that I needed a job, but first I had to work out how to survive.

For a couple of months, I slept on floors and sofas – spaces generously offered by friends and friends-of-friends. Then I moved into squats run by people I'd got to know while visiting Mum in prison. These were small-time criminals who were happy to lend a helping hand to Zoora's daughter. Mum was a vulnerable inmate, clearly out of her depth, with little English and a very timid manner. The working girls liked her and looked out for her. During one visit, I got to know a few of them and one mentioned a place where I could crash. Like Mum, I found myself plunged into a new and very different world – one of sex workers, pimps and petty criminals.

I never talked to Mum about how I was living, as I knew she would have been appalled. Her life was at rock bottom as it was and she certainly didn't need to worry about her homeless daughter. But more significantly, Mum was no longer someone I could turn to – she had lost her role as the protector and nurturer of our family.

Even the fact that Imy was now in Pakistan was not her decision, it was mine. I had become the de facto mother. Mum believed that Foz should remain in Pakistan – she had

Imy with her now, after all. But my siblings were desperate to come home, and thankfully communication had improved by this point. I couldn't risk Foz ending up in another disastrous arranged marriage. In the end, it wasn't up to Mum. It was heart-breaking for us to both tacitly acknowledge that fact.

When you're homeless, you soon find yourself in strange places and awful situations. At one particularly low point, I remember pretending to be asleep on the couch of a filthy squat while two people heated up heroin on tin foil. I'll never forget that sweet, sticky smell – the aroma of despair. I have never succumbed to drugs or alcohol, but when you're homeless and broke, you often have no choice as to where to lay your head. That night, the only place I could find was literally a crack house.

    An older friend of Imy's, Ifty, offered to let me stay at his flat for a few nights, which I gratefully accepted. Ifty didn't have much, but he was happy to share his lodgings. He offered me the tiny spare room, where I slept on a mattress usually reserved for the dog. When Ifty went back to his family to celebrate Eid at the end of Ramadan, I found myself utterly alone. For the first time in my life, I was witnessing Eid without a blood relation or friend to rejoice in the celebrations. Just one person – my cousin Pini – telephoned me to wish me Eid Mubarak. I'll never forget his kindness, nor will I forget the loneliness that swept over me when the call ended and memories of bygone Eids flooded in. It was always a time of great festivity in our household. New outfits and haircuts were a tradition and together we'd cook abundant curries, dahls, samosas and sweet treats. Gifts would change hands before we spent the day visiting friends and family to share the food we had so lovingly prepared.

By contrast, I was now on my own in a strange flat, without a job, my siblings thousands of miles away in Pakistan, my mum a hundred miles away in prison. My dad had newly disowned me for leaving my husband and was nowhere in sight. I didn't have a single person to turn to and I found myself, once again, reaching for a bottle of pills.

Any equanimity I had found after my ten days of contemplation had vanished. I was unable to see a clear path out of this fresh nightmare. Desperate for a little compassion, it seemed clear to me at the time that I had little to live for.

For my mother to function at all in prison, she was prescribed heavy medication. She couldn't put one foot in front of the other without antidepressants and tranquilisers. During Ramadan, Mum fasted as usual, but while she took her meds at dawn with her breakfast, she refused to take them at sundown, believing it was wrong to break her fast with tranquilisers. Mum, like many of our faith, believes there is an absolute obligation to fast during Ramadan. This isn't strictly true – if you are in good health, then yes, fast away, but if you are ailing then an exemption applies without penalty. These days, Ramadan is seen as a month of inner peace, giving and charity. It's a month to reset your balance and thus the balance of the world, to restore and reinvigorate your faith.

During one visit, Mum handed me her unused diazepam to hang on to. These were the pills I reached for now.

I don't remember the details of what happened after I had swallowed all those pills, but I know that Ifty found me and called an ambulance. I know that I ended up in hospital again, having the tranquilisers pumped out of my stomach. In those days there was no counselling, no questions about where I would be heading after I was discharged from hospital. I was on the streets once more, without a soul to turn to, my life saved but my soul in terrible pain.

I was living from one miserable day to the next, not even thinking about what might happen the following week, month or year. All I could focus my weak attention on was getting through the day.

The next time I went to see Mum in prison in Durham, I found out that she'd suffered a reprimand for giving me the diazepam. The hospital had sent a contact report to my next of kin – who happened to be in prison. Seeing her after being discharged from hospital was my wake-up call. I couldn't bring any more pain into her life. I realised that I needed to keep going; that giving up wasn't an option. She looked so sad, so thin, so broken. Now I had added to her despair. Worse, I had made her feel as though she was responsible for what I'd tried to do to myself.

It was a turning point, a lightbulb moment or whatever you want to call it. I knew that I couldn't allow myself to give up – I had to protect Mum. And how would I ever be reunited with my siblings if I didn't pull myself together? How would *they* ever see Mum again without my help? Foz and Imy would be lost to village life, arranged marriages and petty-mindedness. Finally, the lessons of resilience Mum had unknowingly imparted to me over the years kicked in. For good.

My first priority was getting hold of some money for two plane tickets. With renewed resolve, I managed to secure my old job at the mortgage company and began saving almost every penny I made. Still sofa surfing, I didn't have to pay rent, and a nice little nest egg was slowly coming together. Freshly determined to bring my siblings home to start our new lives – which might be very different now – I held on to the dream that soon we would be together again.

9

Bye-Bye Bradford

I wish I could recall for you a happy reunion when I saw Imy and Foz turn the corner into the arrivals hall of Manchester airport. I'm sure we cried, I'm sure we hugged each other. But the truth is, I don't remember. I know I picked them up – these two brave kids who'd flown halfway across the world to come back home to their elder sister – but all I can recall is this grim determination that I had to make sure the three of us survived and hopefully thrived.

When Foz had left Legrams Lane soon after Azam's death, she had waved goodbye to our family sanctuary. If I look back now, particularly through the lens of the leadership lessons I've learnt over the years, I can see how each of us responded so differently to what was in effect the same punishment – the incarceration of our mother, the loss of our home, the fear of having to survive, just the three of us, without any outside support. Those differences have impacted us to this day.

Today, we lead distinct lives, but we've all been shaped by our unique response to the pain of those years. My darling Foz, who found her security ripped out from under her while living thousands of miles away, has always wanted to address that trauma in her own life by making her domestic set-up as safe and secure as possible. Whereas my experience of the trauma was different – I was inside the cauldron while it was burning, and I believe I have emerged with a different priority, one that is more inclined to the notion of not making attachments. I learnt, at the height of our despair, that attachments could make you vulnerable. And Imy, bless him, has perhaps trodden the path in between. With his beautiful house and his kind, loving nature, he has found security in those things he enjoyed before the nightmare began – the nice surroundings and the little treats. The fact that we dealt with the chaos of those years in our own individual ways taught me one very valuable lesson: absolutely every action has a consequence.

I had to make sure we survived, both for the sake of my siblings and for Mum, because, of course, we were just treading water until a miracle might happen and Mum would come home to us. Until then, I blocked out absolutely everything that wasn't going to help us get through each day.

Instinctively, I felt we had to get as far away from Bradford as was practical. Imy and Foz wanted a fresh start too. We were desperate to escape the cloud hanging over our family. Mazhar was still an ever-present threat and I lived in fear that he might track me down and 'punish' me for leaving him. Meanwhile, the three of us continued to be shunned by the entire community. We were the children of a murderer, and the support we had from our wider family was few and far between – Mum's crime had damaged the family izzat even further, if that's possible.

I can still remember, homeless and lost, going to my uncle's house to ask my cousin for help. He turned around and asked me to leave – I was no longer welcome in his house. I went and found a bench in Manningham Park around the corner, where I sat for hours crying in the rain. Crying was as normal to me as breathing in those days; the feelings of rejection were so overwhelming that there was nothing else I could do but despair. This family, interconnected in so many ways through kinship and marriage – my mum's dad and my dad's dad are brothers, after all, and there are so many other supposedly deep ties – this is the close-knit family that slammed the door in our faces. This is the family that didn't care a jot what happened to any of us.

The most immediate problem we had to deal with was the fact that we had nowhere to live. The house in Legrams Lane had been taken by Azam's estate and we had no claim on the property. It felt like I had no choice but to move away. But I couldn't ask my siblings to sleep in squats and crack houses. So, and without any real planning or forethought, I had taken our few belongings to Sheffield before Imy and Foz returned. In the local council office, I explained how we were now parentless and homeless, how I was going to be responsible for a twelve-year-old and a fifteen-year-old, and I was allocated a temporary council flat on the twelfth floor of a block in Beldene Road, which was known locally as 'Thieves' Kitchen'. When I picked them up from the airport, we went straight to the flat.

We were the only people of colour in that block of flats. Soon after we moved in, Imy was jumped by a bunch of white kids in a racist attack. On another occasion, he thought that some boys were looking at Foz the wrong way, so he ushered her into the lift and then came back out to confront them. The poor, brave boy was so skinny that he was beaten up again.

I was aware of all the other mums gathered at the gates, chatting about this and that, the first time I took Foz to her new school. I held myself together for Foz's sake, patted her on the head just like a mum would, told her to have a good day; then I got back into my borrowed old banger and cried my eyes out. These were desperate tears for Foz, because the poor girl didn't have her mum there to wave her goodbye at the school gates. I was crying for her but I was also crying for myself. I was frustrated that I was just trying to do what I thought Mum would want me to do, while in reality not really knowing what I was doing at all. We were such a sad, isolated little trio.

When Foz returned from Pakistan, it wasn't to her mum or to the home she had known in Legrams Lane, but a high-rise in Sheffield. The first time we were all together again with Mum was in Durham Prison. My heart bled for my little sister. She was still a kid.

That evening, we returned to our flat and shared a meal of beans on toast. Each of us was devastated and overwhelmed. Everything crystalised over that meal, everything we had been through hit us all at once. All the furious momentum of our lives paused for a moment, while we sat in silence eating our beans and crying. We all felt the same pain and had no idea how to talk about it. I have no doubt each of us was remembering the last meal we had shared as a family. Facing up to the stark reality that we had gone from that to this.

Ours wasn't a healthy household, and during the misery of our childhoods, talk of suicide was normal in my family. Mum had attempted suicide herself, at the height of what we were later to find out was her horrific abuse. While domestic violence was a taboo subject, suicide – in our house at least – wasn't. Hadn't I, by the age of twenty, attempted to kill myself twice?

And now, so distressed by what had become of our lives, Foz took an overdose of paracetamol. She was just thirteen years old. I can safely say that she wasn't 'copying' me – she had no idea about my own attempts – but that doesn't make me feel any better about how desperate Foz must have been feeling to attempt to take her own life.

Foz isn't like me – I'm an extrovert, but she's slow to trust, and even with me she held back a lot of the turmoil she was suffering. It would also be fair to say that at this point in our lives, I didn't really know her anymore. She had had been a little girl when she left and now, here she was, an adolescent. The structures that had held her life together had vanished, and while we regularly shared an evening meal, we rarely shared our feelings. I had become her mum, without any idea of the child I was supposed to be rearing.

Foz is the most sensitive of all of us. Imy, eldest son of the eldest son, enjoyed an elevated position. He was the favourite boy of the family. I was the black sheep – outspoken, demanding jeans and fringes, despite my lack of a father. If anyone was seen as the victim of our situation it was Imy. It wasn't Foz, and it certainly wasn't me. I was afforded very little leniency, given I had left my husband and strayed from the prescribed path.

We were lucky – Foz survived. But it was an awful wake-up call. As a result of her hospital admittance, we were contacted by social services who gave me a pep talk: *keep going, you're doing really well.*

Really? It's shocking to think back on it all now – two daughters in one family had attempted suicide and it barely raised a single alarm bell. The minute Mum was sentenced to prison, we should have been offered support, also known as 'wraparound care', whereby children are offered care before and after school. But somehow, we had slipped through every net. There was no support, and I was left with two very sad kids.

We never told Mum about Foz's suicide attempt. How could we lay this at her door so soon after my own attempt?

After a couple of months living in Thieves' Kitchen in Sheffield, surviving mostly on Pot Noodles paid for by a weekly benefits grant, we were rehoused by the council into a house in Manor Park. I was still learning how to manage a home, so even though it was a nice new-build council house, we couldn't settle. We were, once again, the only Asians in what was primarily a white area. We did make a few friends, mainly through a video shop in Firth Park where we'd go to rent Bollywood movies to watch at home. There was a guy called Gee who was a boxer, and I asked him to teach Imy how to box so he might be better able to defend himself, should he be jumped again. Gee and his family were kind to us and I'm still in touch with them to this day.

In our desire for order, I established a routine of sorts. I went to work every day and Foz went to school. Imy did mostly what he wanted. My uncle Khadim, our only family member who gave half a damn about us, had given us a mobile phone and regularly sent Mum some money, which took a little of the pressure off our household budget. Even so, there were times we just didn't have the cash to pay for our prison visits.

We had wanted to leave Bradford. We were desperately trying to make a home and create some stability in our lives. We were hungry for routine, structure, a *normal* existence. But we never quite managed it. Running away wasn't going to solve our problems and we were beginning to understand that we took the reality of our lives with us wherever we went.

Given that we were no longer part of an extended family, and family is all-important within the Pakistani community, we struggled to make a home in Sheffield. Despite the new friendships we had forged, there still wasn't quite enough to keep us there.

And so we moved again, this time to Leeds, to an area called Harehills. We didn't fare much better there, so we returned to Sheffield, but this time to an Asian area of the city, which felt much safer. We were allocated a three-bedroom house on Earl Marshal Road and I got a job working in a restaurant called Ayesha's on Ecclesall Road. This was a fancy job – I had to wear a sari. I couldn't get a full-time job because I was responsible for my siblings, and we were also visiting Mum in Durham as often as we could. But at least the restaurant job meant that we could afford a few things for Mum, such as a phone card so we could speak more regularly.

To fill her time in prison, Mum knitted – for England. So there was wool to buy as well. Gradually, aided by the most popular TV soap opera at the time, *Brookside*, Mum's English began to improve, which helped ease her isolation. Even so, Imy, Foz and I just wanted to make sure that she always knew we were there for her, waiting for her; we couldn't bear the idea of her feeling like she'd been abandoned.

These visits were very affectionate and my siblings would be all over Mum, as though they were keeping her safe for the few hours we were together. I, on the other hand, didn't enjoy this sort of physical contact with her – I never had. Being the eldest had something to do with that, but I had had to grow up really fast from the moment my dad left us, and I suppose both my mother and I wanted to cosset Imy and Foz and keep them young and innocent for as long as possible.

In New Hall, the prison Mum was moved back to after Durham, we were granted whole day 'family visits'. Allocated a temporary building, we could spend some private moments away from the antiseptic prison visiting rooms. Mum would prepare samosas in advance and bring them along to the cabin. We'd have breakfast, tea and supper with her. The four of us would snuggle together on the little sofa and watch some TV, each of us trying desperately to recapture a little of the life we'd shared before she was incarcerated. As restrictive as it sounds, we made some good memories during that time.

While she knew we would never abandon her, life inside wasn't easy for Mum. There was the occasional racist abuse hurled at her from some officers, while others were very kind and compassionate, empathising with her vulnerability. Many inmates felt similarly protective towards her. The racism asserted itself through religion and every year there was an issue with Ramadan. Mum was a keen observer, as I mentioned before, but in order to fast all day she would ask to have her breakfast early – traditionally, this would be pre-dawn. Sometimes her request was honoured, but often it wasn't.

While my own faith was yet to assert itself into the kind of devotion it is today, Mum's faith was massively impacted by her time in prison. She began to perform her prayers and finally had time to think about her religion. She was free of Azam's abuse, and in many ways her health improved. She was eating regularly and sleeping without interruption or anxiety. And we siblings helped by never sharing with Mum our own struggles in the outside world. There was an unspoken agreement between us that we would protect her at all costs.

While she was in Durham, Mum worked in the kitchens – a highly prized placement, but then she was an exceptionally well-behaved, category A prisoner, never giving the prison guards any excuse to call her out.

'Your mum's a really good cook!' an inmate called out to us during one visit.

'That,' I told Foz and Imy, 'is Myra Hindley.'

Living in Earl Marshal Road in Sheffield was the first time since Mum's incarceration that the three of us enjoyed some stability. To the Asian families in our area, we explained that our parents currently lived in Pakistan but would soon join us in Sheffield. If we were going to live anonymously, we needed a new story. We believed the fact that our mum was Zoora Shah, the notorious murderer serving time in Durham Prison, wouldn't have drawn any empathy from the Pakistani community. Poor Mum still appeared in the tabloids every now and then – one particularly horrible story detailed how the convicted serial killer Rosemary West was refusing to eat prison food because Mum, the convicted poisoner, was working in the kitchens.

I managed to apply successfully for a grant from the Department of Work and Pensions, which I used to buy a cooker and a set of crockery. I also took out a Credit Union loan, one that would be paid back incrementally from the benefits we were drawing. I bought a blue three-piece suite, which cost me £300, and a set of curtains for the bay windows to match the furniture. We had a rug to cover the floorboards, which I regularly scrubbed on my hands and knees, so obsessed was I with keeping it clean and making a nice home for my siblings. We still couldn't afford to heat the whole house, so we spent most of our time in the front room with the gas fire on. The kitchen was a sorry affair, a chilly space with nothing in it apart from a tiny table and three wonky chairs. Imy didn't even have a bed – he slept on the floor of our bedroom on a pile of charity shop curtains, while Foz and I shared the bed. But at least it was ours; at least we felt safe.

It's a credit to my siblings that they never complained and never once judged me for the way I was managing the household. They rarely asked for things and never challenged my decisions.

I still didn't have Mum's budgeting skills, and to make ends meet I ended up selling the rest of my wedding jewellery. Mum had to have a reasonable allowance and we ended up broke more than once because I was too generous with Imy, trying desperately to make up for the fact I wasn't Mum.

Foz, however, was more resilient. Since her suicide attempt, she had had time to process what had happened to us and also saw that I was doing my best to hold our small family together. While happiness was not yet within our remit, we were growing accustomed to the upheaval in our lives, and, despite the odds, we were bonded to one another, come what may.

My culture dictates that boys hold an elevated position in the family unit and Foz and I felt this very deeply – it had been ingrained in us to protect Imy from the harsh realities that we struggled with every day. When I reflect on this period of my life, I wonder whether I shouldn't have shared more of my burden with my siblings – whether I should have prepared them a little better to cope with all the shit that life threw at us. I have so many regrets about how I disciplined my siblings. I was far too tough, and I very rarely made the space to explore our feelings or nurture a mutual empathy. I exerted power and control over them; I needed Imy and Foz to fall in line and make the best of our shattered lives. It wouldn't be a stretch to say that they feared me a little. They knew they were loved – I made sure of that – but they also knew that my word was law. While we often sat and cried together, we were each isolated in our own misery.

Although Foz had made a friend at school from an Asian family who were kind to us, it was hard for my siblings to settle. While we'd tried to pretend to everyone that we had parents back in Pakistan, before long the truth came out and Foz suffered taunting jibes from her classmates. 'Your mum's a murderer!' they'd scream at her. She'd come home in floods of tears and soon she refused to go to school altogether. While I tried to persuade her to return, I also couldn't bear the thought of her being bullied and harassed for something that was simply just not her fault.

Even though I was trying to protect her, I lacked the instincts and the skills that seemed to come so naturally to my mum. I had no idea what I was doing, let alone how to be a replacement mother for a terrified little girl.

She had already attempted suicide, and this was the final straw. We decided to return to Bradford – while it would be fair to say there would be no one there to eagerly anticipate our return, we figured at least it was familiar and it was the right place to campaign for Mum's release. Maybe the epithet *better the devil you know* would work in our favour for once.

While a social worker was eventually allocated to both Foz and Imy, a lot of damage had already been done. At seventeen, Imy had stopped going to school entirely and was hanging out with a bad crowd and smoking weed. It sounds like we were slowly losing control of our lives, and it's true – we were barely hanging on, just trying to get through one day at a time. Imy's social worker decided that he could try living on his own, but with the support of social services. The idea was that semi-independent living might help him learn the life skills needed for adulthood, such as budgeting and managing a home.

The moment Imy left us, I knew it had been a mistake. I realised I had broken the promise I'd made to myself to keep us together, though I have to acknowledge that there was also a small sense of relief that some of my burden had been lifted – that Imy was no longer part of the equation of chaos that made up our lives. At least I wouldn't have to worry about him. How was I supposed to keep Imy on track and Foz alive?

At this point, I was running on automatic, just putting one foot in front of the other, coping with the next thing life threw at me. As much as I enjoyed dancing, I used these nights out to escape my reality. I was a whirling dervish, moving my body to the music while my mind was enchanted, unfocused and utterly devoid of thought. It was always too brief a respite.

But I had to keep moving forward and my first priority was to make sure Imy stayed out of trouble. I had no guidance on how to do this – my only frame of reference for parenting was my mum. She'd always been a tough disciplinarian, like many of the parents on our street when I was growing up. She wasn't shy about giving me a slap on the arse with her slipper if I was being naughty. She didn't even do it that often, but just frequently enough that when she pointed at her foot and asked, 'Do you remember what size my feet are, Naseem?' that was usually enough to deter me. Things were dealt with differently in those days. So the only real way I knew how to make sure that Imy didn't go completely off the rails was to make him feel guilty and irresponsible.

I had a little speech that I rolled out every time he crossed a line: 'Our mum has lost everything. She's in prison, and your behaviour might land you in jail too. And if it does, I ain't coming to see you. You'll be on your own, mister. And I promise that if that happens you will have nothing to do with our mother, because she deserves a dutiful son. After everything that she's sacrificed for us, we need to stand by her. All three of us. Whenever our mum comes home, she needs to be able to hold her head high, and the only way she'll be able to do that is if her kids are faultless.'

If I had one skill back then, it was hardnosed emotional blackmail. What else could I do? There was no one around to give me any better advice. It was like taking a sledgehammer to crack a nut at times, but it worked and Imy pulled himself together. He never once challenged these mini lectures, as it wasn't the done thing in our culture – your elders will always get the final word, and you had better keep your eyes on the ground while said lecture is being pronounced.

Around this time, it would be fair to say that there were a handful of very precious people who extended the hand of friendship. Mum's old friend from Leeds, Baji Shamim, looked out for us, even though members of her own family warned her not to have anything to do with us. There were others, too, who invited the three of us to celebrate Eid with them. This gesture was so important to us, given our own extended family wanted nothing to do with us. To be invited into friends' homes to celebrate Ramadan felt almost magical. Gradually, as the months and then years went by, one or two cousins and uncles and aunties reached out to us. But there was one person, my uncle Khadim – my mum's first cousin in Luton – who was consistently there for us. Khadim was a proper Yorkshireman who worked his whole life at Vauxhall car makers. Recognising we had been abandoned, he stepped in and stepped up, visiting frequently and helping out where he could. As well as buying us mobile phones, he paid the phone bills. He visited my mum regularly and even contributed towards her allowance – and ours when we were struggling. In the desert of our family, Khadim was a consistent friend, always ready with kind words and unwavering support during those traumatic years.

We did have another cousin, Mahmood, who is now a successful academic and was studying in Sheffield while we were living there. He would rock up every so often and buy us pizza, which was amazing because we couldn't afford to buy it ourselves.

*

Although we had proved we could survive outside our community, Bradford was our home. Yes, the Shahs might have been a shameful family, but it was still the only place we felt we entirely belonged, and where my mother would return to when she was released. While it was obvious we would find our way home one day, we couldn't have anticipated the bombshell that would send us straight back to the city we'd grown up in.

10

Southall Black Sisters

Bang!

Imy punched his fist into the windscreen so hard I have no idea how it didn't shatter. It was only a little Ford Fiesta, which my dad's brother, Pav, had loaned to me so I could drive us up to New Hall to see Mum. The noise of the impact was like a car crash, and if the windscreen was still intact then Imy surely must have fractured his hand. But I didn't even think to ask him about his hand – I was crying so hard, all while trying to control a moving car. Foz was sobbing in the back seat.

It was 1996, Foz and I had been attending meetings at the home of Rahila Gupta, one of the members of the women's organisation Southall Black Sisters – a non-profit advocacy group that helps Black and minoritised women live free from all forms of violence and abuse.

Imy hadn't known about these meetings, and I had chosen this moment – in the car – to tell him exactly what we had found out during these sessions with Rahila.

It was Mum who had initiated contact with Southall Black Sisters several months earlier. She had heard about the case of Kiranjit Aluwalia, an Indian-born woman of Sikh heritage who had been imprisoned in the UK in 1989 after killing her husband. In 1992, after a long intervention by Pragna Patel and her colleagues at Southall Black Sisters, Kiranjit's case had come up for appeal and her long history of abuse at the hands of her husband had come to light for the first time. As a result, her conviction was changed from murder to manslaughter on the grounds of diminished responsibility.

Mum learnt of the case while in Durham and reached out to the organisation to request a visit. She had been in prison for two years by this point.

Pragna Patel, one of the remarkable women who set up the charitable group, began to visit Mum in Durham, initially without our knowledge. It's important to note that at the time, I was still of the belief that Mum was entirely innocent of anything to do with Azam's death; despite the forensic evidence, I still believed it was a miscarriage of justice and that he had died from natural causes. My mum was no murderer.

Pragna, however, realised that there was more to Mum's story than met the eye. She knew the forensics couldn't lie, and that Mum had obviously poisoned Azam. But what could drive a timid woman like Zoora Shah to do such a thing? Pragna's years of experience working with vulnerable and abused women had given her the insight that I just didn't have as a naive 22-year-old. She was keen to probe the depths of Mum's story, the horrific abuse she had suffered at Azam's hands, the numerous abortions, the sexually transmitted diseases, the pimping out of her body.

Slowly, visit by visit, Pragna pieced together the facts behind the headlines.

Foz and I were summoned. Listening to her as she recounted Mum's experiences was like an out-of-body experience. We were being asked to take everything we had believed about Mum's case and to dismiss it, to accept a new truth. A truth so seismic that both Foz and I barely breathed a word as Pragna explained Mum's side of the story.

The shock of my mother's actions aside, I still thought of Azam as *Uncle* Azam. But now a puzzle was coming together before my eyes, piece by tiny piece. Once we had the full story, Mum's behaviour made sense – it was like wiping a dirty window clean and seeing through to the other side, to the truth. I finally understood Mum's withdrawal, her preoccupation and desperate anxiety.

I could finally see Azam's behaviour through a new lens.

Azam had never liked our relatives and made his opinion of them clear. According to him, they were interfering, small-minded and didn't have our best interests at heart. But now I saw how his words were aimed at isolating our mother from her support network. It would be far easier to exert control over her if no one else was around to point out just how sinister his presence was. He was very kind to me and my siblings, too – bringing groceries, giving us money – and in this way he was also controlling us. If we liked Azam, why would we question the fact he was always at our house, commandeering all Mum's attention? I cherished his company much of the time – he was my uncle and he had our backs. And didn't we have him to thank for the security of Legrams Lane and saving us from schlepping around the city, renting cold rooms with outside loos?

All these mind games guaranteed Azam could carry on doing what he was doing to Mum with impunity.

As I listened to Pragna, I recalled the times I'd watch Mum

huddled by the gas fire of an evening, crying. At the time, this wasn't an unfamiliar sight; her burden of being a single mother of three children weighed heavily on us as well. Now, Foz and I could see it was because she was a victim of abuse – she had felt destitute, isolated and desperate, beyond the struggles of our daily lives as an ostracised and fatherless family.

It finally made sense that Mum was where she was, serving a prison sentence for killing a man. The fact that she had murdered Azam hadn't changed, but we had the context of abuse and violence in which to reframe her actions.

Now it was time to unpack the forensic evidence and the reasons why Mum had put arsenic into Azam's food. And this, too, came to light. Mum had believed in the old folk remedy of a small dose of arsenic to safely lower a man's libido. She had sourced the powder on a visit to Pakistan, having no idea it was poisonous.

Pragna was the very first soul Mum had spoken to about her life with Azam and what he had demanded of her. But despite her confession, Mum was still very resistant to the idea of an appeal for the very same reason she had maintained her silence during the trial: fear of losing her izzat.

Can you imagine the impact of this news, after Pragna informed us?

At that point, Imy wasn't in a strong enough place to process such traumatic information, which was why Foz and I decided not to share it with him. At least, not yet. But for me and my sister, it was absolutely devastating. Neither of us had the remotest idea that the man we thought of as Uncle Azam had in fact been a sick, violent, psychotic abuser and that our Mum – who for years had acted so strangely that I had occasionally resented her – had suffered in silence because she thought she was protecting us from the shame of her dishonour.

In all kinds of ways, I am still processing the shock of that revelation back in 1995. And I suspect I will be processing it for the rest of my life.

But once I did know, there was no way I could accept that Mum would surrender potential freedom for the sake of izzat. As I've said before, izzat is a very complex concept. When a woman has been killed by a man in a so-called 'honour killing', the man can perversely claim that he was protecting his own family's izzat by punishing the woman who had stepped out of line and shamed the family by exercising what she considered her right to behave as she wished. Yet if a woman – let's say my mum – killed a man because for years he had horrifically abused her, she could incur the loss of her own izzat. What could Mum have done differently? Well, the community might respond, she could have just put up with it.

To make it even more complicated, the wish to gain and maintain my own izzat has, I freely admit, been one of the driving forces throughout my life. It is the compass by which I have navigated my own success, against all the odds. I can list for you the number of ways, even now, in which I constantly attempt to maintain my izzat. For example, if you come to my house, you will always be offered food, which I will insist on making for you myself: in my culture, being hospitable and feeding our guests is a fundamental teaching of Islam. Izzat is part of my status as a politician, a representative of the people of Bradford West, and I take enormous pride in that. Rightly or wrongly, wealth and material gain are to some extent a reflection of success and, while I am certainly not a wealthy woman, the fact that I drive a decent car and have a house with a mortgage which provides a roof over my kids' heads is a part of my own izzat.

But, more often than not, izzat is defined by the behaviour of women. Women must act according to the social rules set by men for the purposes of men – and these rules are encoded into a standard of behaviour used to exert power and control over women.

Mum had been sentenced to twenty years behind bars and was now effectively telling me that she would rather this unconscionable situation continue, with her children struggling to survive on their own, than suffer the shame of her izzat being compromised by having her ordeal exposed to the world. She had wanted to talk to Southall Black Sisters to see what help they might offer to end this nightmare, but revealing the details of her abuse to the world was a different story.

Clearly, I had to talk to her.

'Whose izzat are you trying to protect exactly?' I asked her. 'Your brothers' izzat? Those same brothers who failed to take care of you and your children when your husband, their cousin, abandoned you? Who insisted you give up your children to your adulterous husband. Or the izzat of the wider Shah family, the ones who left you at the mercy of a world which you didn't understand, in a foreign country whose language you didn't speak?'

I asked Mum, where was the honour of the men in my family? This izzat, this code of behaviour, clearly didn't apply to them. Why? Because they were men! But according to the rules of patriarchy, weren't men supposed to look out for their women?

'So tell me, Mum,' I went on, fully in my stride. 'These people you think you are shielding with your silence, are they the ones who're suffering? It's us who are suffering. It's you, in this prison. It's your children making their own way in the world without their mother. We want you at home with us. That's the end of it.'

'Baj is right, Mum,' chimed in Foz. 'You're prepared to keep quiet to protect those who don't care about us, to protect their izzat. You're not the only one doing time. We are living through your sentence too. Don't you have an obligation to your children? We've have lost our mother, and you have put your family before your kids for the sake of izzat. And they don't even care about you. If they'd have been there for you, you would never be in this position. It's time to put us first.'

I see now that we were putting Mum under an enormous amount of pressure to go against her conditioning. She was being asked to challenge her deeply ingrained belief in the correct code of conduct, in honour and izzat. Here were her kids, telling her to simply forget all about that and tell the world her true story.

You see this sort of misplaced loyalty in Bollywood films, where the family might disown a daughter who has made an inappropriate marriage. You then witness the family desperately missing their child. Who is the winner in this scenario? What a shabby kind of honour it is to cause such a seismic rift in a loving family. Eventually, a reconciliation will take place, and while the ending of the movie is happy enough, the needless pain and suffering are incomprehensible.

Eventually, and with much trepidation – but also now with genuine anger at the way in which her life had unfolded – Mum came to the decision herself that she wanted to speak up.

And that's how the campaign to secure her release started, led by those amazing women from Southall Black Sisters. Now, with Mum's approval, we were able to glimpse a future where we might – just might – be able to overturn that cruel prison sentence.

It strikes me now, as I pick my way through those strange, emotionally turbulent times, just how many cycles were being repeated, just how many patterns of behaviour I myself was unconsciously replicating. It was the women of Southall Black Sisters, after Mum had reached out to them, who enabled her to finally give new meaning to her case. And it was the women of the family, Foz and I, who had to absorb these revelations first. I can say now that Imy wasn't in a good enough place mentally to hear the information that we had started to receive from Pragna, but looking back, I wonder why we had come to this conclusion. After all, why would Foz – a fifteen-year-old girl – be able to deal with the explicit abuse Mum suffered at the hands of Azam and his horrible mates, and not Imy? How brave was my Foz then, how courageous she was to sit with me during those sessions, listening to the stories Mum recounted about being raped by Azam beside the graves of her own dead children.

In reality, we ourselves were perpetuating the patriarchal notion that women should suck up the pain while the men go about their daily business. That's not Imy's fault – he didn't know anything about it, because we chose not to tell him the terrible details of Mum's abuse. And why was that? Because all of us – Mum, Foz, Southall Black Sisters, me – by tacit acknowledgement, believed that it was up to the women to deal with the emotional realities of life. To sort everything out without 'needlessly' involving the men – or rather, 'sparing' the men.

My sister is an amazing woman in all kinds of ways. Looking back, I realise just how amazing a young girl she was, too, to stand so tall during those dark, revelatory days.

Eventually, we had to tell Imy the truth. We also had to own up to the fact that we'd been privy to this information for months. Telling him while manoeuvring a car round a roundabout to get onto the M606 – probably not a great idea. But when was going to be the right time to tell my teenage brother that his mum had been sexually abused and exploited by Uncle Azam and many other men?

Coming from a community where periods and sex are still not openly discussed, let alone abuse and exploitation, I knew I couldn't just have this conversation sat around at home. It was too hard. But Imy had to know what had happened to our mum; we had to tell him we were going to fight for her release and that every horrible detail would soon be in the public domain. That her plight, if you saw it from my perspective, or the dirty laundry – if you saw it through the lens of izzat and patriarchy – was the whole basis of the appeal. I needed Imy on side, because out of all of us, it would be hardest for him to bear the publicity – simply because he was a man.

Telling him in the car was my way of orchestrating a managed response. I thought it might be somewhere where my brother wouldn't go crazy and smash his head against a wall or throw food. I suspected there would be tears and anger, but I certainly didn't expect that punch to the windscreen.

In seconds we were all crying. For me and Foz, a burden had been lifted. We had been so worried about how Imy would take the news, so it was a relief it was finally out there.

It was, of course, a terrible journey, but now at least we were all on the same page and could begin to plan our next move.

11

The Birth of an Activist

Now that we knew the truth, we had a different future to look forward to. A future where it might – just might – be possible to secure Mum's release.

Pragna and Mum's lawyers were very careful to manage our expectations, and they soon made me realise just how heavily the justice system was skewed against the lived realities of a non-English-speaking Pakistani woman like Mum. They were joined by another genuinely remarkable woman, Jude Boyles, from the voluntary group Justice for Women, a feminist law-reform organisation that campaigns against legislation that discriminates against women in cases involving male violence against partners. Jude provided case support as well as supporting me and my siblings. To this day, she remains one of my closest, most respected and beloved friends. There were many other brilliant and powerful women who were congregating to offer much-needed advice, including Julie Bindel and Harriet Wistrich, the co-founders of Justice for Women.

Meanwhile, the landscape of our lives was changing. More significantly for me, through my exposure to the interventions by Pragna, Hannana Siddiqui and Meena Patel at SBS, as well as Jude, I began to absorb the lessons of campaigning. I became a sponge for this new flow of information about how the world operated, and how one might try to change it. I had never spent a second considering such concepts before, but now I was all ears as powerful and knowledgeable women explained the processes, systems and methods that could be harnessed to tackle injustice.

I felt some optimism for the first time since Mum had been arrested. The forensics said one thing, but up to that fateful dinner, Mum was saying another. Since Mum's confession, it seemed that both stories could be true. Yes, Mum had killed Azam, but it was also true that she wasn't a bad person. Finally, we had some context for her actions.

I was twenty-two years old and at times it felt like I was taking a PhD in violence against women, about inequality and how the justice system was skewed against women.

The whole concept of injustice had never occurred to me before. I had always followed my mum's example, kept my head down, bought my copy of the *Sun* and my fags, gone out to work at the crisps factory every day or woken up every morning in Hamidabad Colony in Pakistan knowing that I had duties to perform. It never, for a moment, crossed my mind that I might direct my energies towards grand concepts like justice, politics and equality. That someone like me could make a difference.

You might look at my early years and say that, yes, I did react to injustice. Instinctively, I knew I had to leave Mazhar, that I couldn't just put up with a toxic marriage. Instinctively, I knew that my father's abuse and subsequent abandonment of his children wasn't fair on my mum. Instinctively, I knew we should have been offered support after Mum's incarceration.

THE BIRTH OF AN ACTIVIST

But while these were knee-jerk reactions to 'unfairness' in my eyes, I never framed it all within the wider context of justice. I had little idea that all these events reflected varying degrees of misogyny, of women's inequality, of injustice.

However, I'm a quick learner. I've always winged it where exams are concerned, because I've got a funny brain that lets me process information extremely quickly. It can be quite off-putting to my political colleagues and adversaries – I'm constantly aware of the undercurrent of sexist, racist and downright patronising behaviour, and when this brown woman opens her mouth and makes it obvious she's grasped what's going on around her, it can make people feel uncomfortable. Which is a good thing, by the way!

I began to think about Mum's past and her current situation in a broader light, situating her experiences using new language and a new awareness. My own language changed to take power, abuse and control into my lexicon. I needed to be able to process this information quickly, because it soon became obvious that I was going to have to become the public face of the emerging campaign to launch an appeal against Mum's conviction. Southall Black Sisters, Justice for Women and a host of legal advisors would provide the ammunition for the campaign, which was run by her lawyer, Rohit Sanghvi, but there would need to be a figurehead, and it was obvious that I would need to step up to the mark.

On a more practical note, we needed to move back to Bradford.

We realised that if we were going to build a campaign for Mum's release, we had to be in the city where it all happened. Imy gave up his flat to join us and the council found us a place to live – Cranmer House. Imy had realised he wanted the stability of family life, and it would help to have a male presence in the house, no matter how much I rebelled against the patriarchy.

We hauled our precious three-piece suite back from Sheffield and set up home in the maisonette. This time there would be no question of abandoning the top floor because we couldn't afford to heat it. This time we had a proper gas stove and we were finally able to start cooking the sort of food our mum used to make. We bought big bags of chapati flour and Foz and I would use the skills we'd learnt in Pakistan to make chapatis and parathas with which we'd mop up our dahl, once in a while splashing out on some lamb or chicken to make a proper meat curry.

We were infused with optimism. We had a goal to aim for and this drew us closer than ever. Given that Mum wasn't coming home any time soon, it was the push we needed to sort out our lives and prepare a secure base for when she did return. We had been unstable for too long, and now we had some structure to our lives. Gone were the days of merely surviving, of living from one prison visit to the next. With a bounce in our step, a less bleak future was within our reach.

Imy got a job in a car-parts factory, and I found Foz a school to attend, where she found her tribe. In the sixth form, she would meet her husband-to-be.

Foz's school had a further education division and I enrolled myself on the Certificate for Mature Students course, which would lead to a qualification equivalent to GCSEs and A levels. I still had university in my sights; I knew I needed to sort out my life and education was key. For the first time in a

THE BIRTH OF AN ACTIVIST

long time, too, we had some close family support: Uncle Pav, Dad's brother who had loaned me his Fiesta, was in Bradford with his partner, Mitzi, and their little daughter, Sasha. With them we enjoyed the first normal family interaction since Mum's arrest.

Now, with our focus on building an appeal case for Mum, it was time for me to take up my role as the public face of the campaign. Southall Black Sisters had appointed a colleague to run the campaign in Bradford and I was due to give my first speech at Bradford College. During my presentation, I cried so much my tears blurred the words of my handwritten speech and I barely made it to the end. But the more I spoke, the more confidence I gained to campaign harder. Our message was clear: yes, Mum had administered the fatal dose of poison to Azam, but she should have been convicted of manslaughter owing to diminished responsibility, not murder, and therefore shouldn't have received the draconian sentence of twenty years.

Over a period of eighteen months while we lobbied for an appeal, I attended and took part in events organised by Southall Black Sisters to build campaign momentum. Although unaware at the time, I was beginning to understand how campaigning and lobbying were key to challenging racism and inequality. I had a new skillset, one that money couldn't buy. It's true that college can give you an education, but it can't teach you how to engage actively with inequality. I found myself in conversations with women at the top of their game, serious activists who were always ready to offer their support. And then I began to run with my newfound self-assurance. And why not?

My expertise had evolved from my lived experience – it

was authentic. If you can use your personal experience for the benefit of wider society and see results, you're a successful activist. You have recognised that your issues don't exist in isolation but are shared by many. Successful activism is about translating the lived experience to show how these issues affect everyone, reflecting a universal injustice. I began to understand women are confined to certain roles within society: they are expected to be faithful nurturers, willing empathisers and passive observers. But, if they step out of line, we punish them *harder* than men, because their transgressions go against their perceived 'nature'. We expect men to misbehave, so we are more lenient when they do. Now I had been exposed to systemic injustice, I would never be able to unsee it.

I travelled to London to speak at events, where I would tell our story over and over again. I even appeared on TV on the *Richard & Judy* show to make the case for Mum.

Our campaign was about lobbying powerful support, and this included the support of trade unions. I stood up at the TUC (Trade Union Congress) conference and spoke of our campaign. Alone, on a podium overlooking an audience of thousands, I told Mum's story. It was daunting, yes, but that day was a success and now we had the unions on side.

I learnt how to control my emotions when speaking publicly, even though I often collapsed into tears straight afterwards. I listened carefully to the arguments our team was building, and I discovered that I was effective at getting important and often complicated points over clearly.

And to manage my stress I was dancing more than ever, five nights a week if I could manage it and I didn't care what anyone thought.

THE BIRTH OF AN ACTIVIST

I had to develop a thick skin very quickly. In order to defend Mum, I had to wash our family's dirty laundry in public. If I was going to convince people that Mum's life had been so intolerable that she had felt compelled to take drastic and, yes, criminal, action – well, if I was going to stand a chance of defending her and being heard – I needed everyone to know exactly what she had endured. That's a tough call for any daughter, but even more challenging given the culture in which I was raised. A largely patriarchal culture where violence against women was never openly acknowledged.

Mum had had several abortions during the period of her abuse and in order to represent her in the campaign I had to somehow reconcile to myself – never mind the family and community – that while my cultural conditioning dictated that abortion was a sin, I could understand why my mother had gone through with the procedure, and multiple times no less. It's hard to believe that it even occurred to her to have an abortion, given her own conditioning. It became clear to me as I campaigned that the truth was more important than any preconceived notions of what was right or wrong. The facts had changed, and therefore we, too, had to shift our thinking. Our framework for understanding the world had to be adjusted and we had to fight our cognitive dissonance. We used to believe that any affair outside marriage is *haram* (forbidden) and yet my mother had engaged in one. But then I also understood her vulnerability, that she was being pimped and abused. There wasn't nearly enough time to process this influx of new thinking properly, but we had to do so nonetheless. A man was dead, Mum was in prison – those facts hadn't changed. But the context of these events reshaped the narrative.

Imy, Foz and I struggled sometimes with these disclosures. It's very, very hard to have your mother spoken about in public in this way. But I knew that this was the only way in which she might be able to secure her freedom. I also knew, now that I was able to talk to her about it when I visited her, that this was what she wanted me to do. We never once discussed the details of her abuse – the most she would tell me was that Azam wasn't a 'nice man' – but she knew that Pragna had given me chapter and verse. Mum couldn't talk to me then, and hasn't opened up to me since, about her ordeal. It's just too painful. But, once she had taken the decision to speak, she never wavered in her determination that the truth should be told. Mum is a proud woman; the genie was out of the bottle, and she wanted me to make sure the whole world knew what she'd been through.

We needed to be transparent about Mum's experiences in order to back up the arguments we were assembling for the forthcoming appeal. The case that was finally made on Mum's behalf consisted of several strands. The first was that the legal definition of 'domestic violence' in the 1990s was still restricted to physical violence within marriage. It didn't cover other elements of coercive control such as economic domination. What Mum's case clearly demonstrated was that a woman could be abused in a host of ways beyond physical violence. Also at play was the fact that at the original court hearing, Mum had been asked why she hadn't tried to seek help from the police or her GP while she was being terrorised by Azam. But this failed to take into account the complexity of patriarchal control and the power of izzat within the British Pakistani community, effectively showing how out of touch the white British judicial system was with the lived realities of ethnic British families.

Azam's brother was a powerful religious and community leader in Bradford, and the court had entirely failed to assess the impact which that status might have on a lone woman like Mum and her ability to stand up for herself. The appeal would address the central issue that her use of poison wasn't the act of a cunning and manipulative murderer, but the tragic attempt by a helpless woman to curb the sex drive of the man who was tormenting her. She had believed it was a traditional folk remedy.

In those days, the British legal system was still shot through with male assumptions about domestic violence and women's responses to such abuse. The system couldn't distinguish between those who kill out of self-interest and power, and those who do so out of despair born of the impoverished and oppressive conditions of their lives.

We wouldn't claim Mum didn't kill Azam. Instead, we put forward that the conditions of her life and the state of her mental health after so many years of poverty and abuse led her to commit manslaughter. We would claim that she had already suffered enough and should be released.

In so many ways, my horizons now seemed to stretch far ahead of me, while before they had always been limited to the familiar narrow, blackened sandstone streets of Bradford. We used to have campaign meetings in Pragna's flat in northwest London and occasionally at Rahila Gupta's house. I loved to visit Rahila's house, because, to me, it was the height of luxury, a designer's dream home, with its fitted kitchen and matching dining table and chairs.

I'd never visited such a posh house before. At the time, Imy and Foz and I were still living in one room in Earl Marshal Road in Sheffield with our solitary electric hob standing on its own in the kitchen. After every visit to Rahila's house, with its seaside-themed bathroom and mosaic tiles decorated with fish, I'd think to myself, *I want a bathroom just like that one day.*

I began to use my emerging awareness of the power of campaigning to think about other cases. Stephen Lawrence was murdered by white racists in London in 1993 and I started to follow his brave mother Baroness Doreen Lawrence's campaign to seek justice for her son. I became enraged when Mum was denied halal meat at New Hall Prison and staged a protest outside the gates. Legally, the prison was obliged to accommodate the dietary requirements of its inmates. It's one thing going to a school and not having halal meat on the menu, because it's readily available at home, but Mum and other Muslim prisoners don't have the same choices. They are in prison every day for twenty-four hours a day. The campaign was successful.

The more I learnt about systemic inequality, the more I felt empowered to challenge the restrictive structures in place. I'd had enough of being on the receiving end of unfairness – I was taking charge. This was a huge shift in how I perceived the world, and using my energy now to protest, instead of watching and suffering on the sidelines, felt invigorating and purposeful. Life was a hustle, but I felt useful and inspired.

THE BIRTH OF AN ACTIVIST

These days, my hustling is different because I have a mandate and my voice is elevated, but the principles remain the same.

I staged another protest when Mum was prevented from observing Ramadan in the correct way, being told she wasn't allowed to break her fast at sunset because it didn't accord with the mealtime regime. Today, many cultural and religious observances are supported in British jails, but when Mum was locked up, it was a constant battle to allow her these few shreds of dignity.

While the petty bureaucracy of the prison system initially intimidated me, before long I was standing up for our rights as visitors whenever the prison officers tried to create difficulties. Once, upon our arrival at Durham Prison, we were told by some bumptious official that Mum could only have one visitor that day. Because Mum couldn't write, helpful officers would help her fill out her visiting card, by suggesting she write down the name of only one of her children and use ditto marks for her other two children. Unhelpful screws (I'm afraid that's how we referred to prison officers) would deliberately ignore the ditto marks and say only one visitor was marked down, so only one would be allowed in. That battle I didn't win and Foz and I waited in the car while Imy went in to see Mum.

While we were living in Cranmer House in Bradford, not far from the city centre, and after I'd been working on the campaign for several months, I began volunteering for the Samaritans. Maybe I would pursue a career within the social services/care sector – I could already sense how this kind of work might provide a positive outlet for the anger I felt over

Mum's treatment in prison and at the hands of men like Azam. I suspected that the Samaritans would provide a new way for me to engage with those who needed help. Mum had always gone out of her way to assist every waif and stray that crossed her path and perhaps subconsciously, I was trying to follow her example. By this point I was much more familiar with the concepts of justice, fairness and equality, but I was sure I didn't want to pursue a career in women's rights. I was reluctant to focus on domestic violence, despite my high profile in this area due to the campaign.

My narrative at the time was that I didn't want to be known as the woman who used her mum's campaign as a platform for her own career, and perhaps I was overly sensitive about establishing an identity separate from Mum's appeal. These days, I can't stress enough that the best campaigns are born out of personal experience. No doubt about it.

The campaign was gaining momentum, and in January 1998, the renowned journalist Duncan Campbell wrote a very powerful feature in the *Guardian* about Mum's case, headlined 'Despair drove woman to kill'. The word was spreading and I was invited to speak at more and more events. The local papers were also starting to run stories about the appeal, rather than just salacious titbits about my mum the murderer.

As the date for the appeal in April of that year drew closer, despite everyone in the team urging me to remain open-minded about the outcome, I felt sure that all our efforts would prove worthwhile. I genuinely could not imagine how anyone, whether prestigious High Court judge or person in the street, couldn't see that Mum had committed her crime out of desperation rather than malice.

She had been behind bars for over four years at this point, mostly in Durham Prison, but in the run-up to the case review she had been moved to the notorious women's prison in London, Holloway.

She'd done her time, hadn't she? Didn't she deserve a break, after all that unhappiness?

12

A Broken Woman

On the last day of April 1998, the Court of Appeal dismissed Mum's appeal against her conviction for murder. Apparently, she didn't deserve a break.

A two-minute phone call with the solicitor was all it took to bring our world crashing down once more.

Nothing made sense to me. The case had been so strong, so definitive in its exposure of Mum's abuse and now, in what felt like a parallel dimension, justice had been withheld. My mother was to remain in prison.

Lord Justice Kennedy had presided over the appeal, sitting with Mr Justice Butterfield and Mr Justice Richards. Lord Justice Kennedy summarised their reasoning with brutal clarity: 'By her own admission, she has lied repeatedly in the past, and we are far from satisfied that she has ceased to do so.' The judges couldn't understand why Mum hadn't sought help if her life had been as awful as she'd claimed, and seemed to believe that it was surely just a simple matter for her to report Azam to the police or confide in a professional advisor. The fact that Mum hadn't done so only pointed, they appeared to conclude, to her guilt. And why at her original trial, they asked, had Mum denied killing Azam, when now she was prepared to admit to it on the grounds of diminished responsibility?

To me, and to many others, it seemed like the three white judges were looking down upon Mum from a great height, so distant were they from the realities of her life. It was as though they couldn't begin to empathise with a situation so radically at odds with their own understanding and experience of how people engaged with one another. All the work we had put into the case to try to explain cultural codes such as izzat and honour within our community, and how patriarchal structures meant that women like Mum didn't have the luxury of going to the police – none of that seemed to matter at all. It was as though it was all just irrelevant chatter compared to the precise reasoning of the law.

Following the decision, Southall Black Sisters put out a statement declaring that: 'Male prejudice and lack of compassion for women who suffer domestic violence is alive and well in the legal profession.'

From my experience of listening to the women who built the campaign for Mum over the past eighteen months, I was now confident in my understanding of the wider social and political frameworks that surrounded both her conviction and the rejection of her appeal. I had absorbed a huge wealth of knowledge about how the world actually worked for disadvantaged people and so I could completely understand the perspective that lay behind that rejection. Mum had lost her appeal because of male prejudice and lack of empathy. But at the same time, for me, it was deeply personal.

I was devastated.

Following the verdict, Imy got on the phone to a friend: 'Mate, you need to take Naz out dancing. She's going crazy.' And so, for a few hours I lost myself in music, entering that trance-like state, where nothing beyond moving my body to the rhythms of R&B and house music mattered.

It would be fair to say my life juddered to a halt that day. The two years I'd spent at the adult education centre were aimed at qualifications I would need to carry on with my studies. I'd been planning to take a course in psychology and counselling at Bradford and Ilkley Community College, which could set me up for a career working in the sector. It was over; it didn't even cross my mind to take the final exams and I dropped out. I felt flat and demotivated, deciding it was time to focus on earning a living while dedicating my spare time to working towards a reduction in Mum's sentence.

It would also be fair to say that there had been one positive outcome of that horrible day when Mum's hope was extinguished. I realised then that advocacy, campaigning, politics – whatever you want to call it – must be always and absolutely centred on the reality of a person's lived experience.

To this day, everything I try to achieve within the world of politics is based upon that principle: that behind every word which we as political representatives and leaders utter must lie the solid foundation of real human experience. I'd witnessed what I considered to be justice devoid of context. I'd witnessed a cruel and antiseptic application of the law without thought for the human being concerned. I would never forget the bitter lesson of the day Mum's appeal was dismissed – nor would I forget the lessons it taught me.

I was still volunteering for the Samaritans at the time and there I learnt another valuable lesson that I know will see me through the rest of my life: we must always show compassion and empathy towards others. If we don't share the lived experience of those in trouble, then it's our duty to at least try to empathise. When they are sunk deep into the pit of despair, those who are suffering need a crutch – why not provide that crutch if it's within our remit?

The judges deciding on Mum's appeal made little effort to understand who my mother was, or where she had come from. They had no interest in her cultural heritage and how that might have impacted the choices she had made. Her life bore little resemblance to the lives of those responsible for pronouncing judgment upon her, and in the end that counted against her. Given the lack of compassion for her situation or empathy for her actions, perhaps the verdict shouldn't have been such a surprise.

Had she been arrested by a woman, Mum's experience might have been different. Had she been arrested by a brown woman, it might have been different again. Had she been arrested by a woman of her own culture, from the very start Mum would have been shown at least a little compassion.

As an Asian woman, Pragna understood the meaning of izzat and realised there was more to this case than the tabloids would have anyone know.

While it was a devastating blow for us, life had to go on. We had bared our souls. We had shared Mum's guilt, her shame, her abuse – and it hadn't worked. By this point Mum had already been in prison for six years. We had to galvanise ourselves to secure her a reduced tariff. We needed a new campaign.

With Mum still inside, but now at New Hall Prison outside

Wakefield, the three of us just had to make the best of it. Imy was still working at the car-parts factory and had plans to move back to Sheffield for a while. Perhaps, understandably, he wanted a break from it all – a break from us, from this fresh trauma and the meetings and the noise of the campaign. Foz, meanwhile, had grown up too; she had left school and was studying at sixth form college. She met a young lad, Pav, who was holding down a decent job at Morrisons in Bradford and had his eyes set on buying his own house. They became engaged and shortly after that, they got married. All these years later, they're living in a lovely house with their kids not far from where I'm writing this book in Bradford.

With Imy in Sheffield and Foz married to Pav, I was on my own again. In March 1999, I rented a cottage from one of my Samaritans colleagues in Little Horton Lane. I had put my education on hold for the moment, deciding that I had so much life experience that I didn't necessarily need qualifications to secure good employment and a career path.

My first stop was with Bradford social services as a residential social worker working with kids with autism, and then at the Black Women's Support Project, supporting vulnerable and abused women.

It was easier to see Mum now that she was at New Hall, but every visit was still painful. She seemed to be shrinking. Listless as she was, it was only her knitting that kept her going, and I was saving as much money as I could to buy wool.

By the time her appeal came round, Mum had been in prison for six years. That's a long time to be away. When she was first arrested, she was ostracised by a huge section of the community and wider family, but the new revelations at the appeal isolated her even further. Talking about sex is taboo, and having your sex life splashed across the front pages of the daily newspapers was beyond comprehension for them. But Mum never let the familial isolation defeat her. She got along with everyone in prison, sharing what she could – biscuits, food, money and her time with those she befriended. She didn't drink or smoke and her obvious vulnerability seemed to endear her to her fellow inmates. As well as knitting, Mum prayed, her faith growing stronger and stronger.

With the appeal behind us, the focus of our efforts was now on the Home Secretary of the day, Jack Straw, to whom we would present our case and make the plea to reduce the original prison tariff of twenty years. I was pretty battle-hardened by this point, so I didn't allow my own expectations to get the better of me. Instead, I concentrated my efforts on putting one foot in front of the other, working hard and building a petition to present to Mr Straw.

Maybe as a result of our crashing disappointment, it seemed like the best way to attempt to secure the right decision from the Home Office was to zero in on human communication. Our campaign shifted focus with a new strategy; we would encourage supporters to write personal letters expressing their thoughts and feelings about Mum's case once they had learnt all that she had endured, all that she had lost.

Perhaps one of the most powerful letters came from an unexpected quarter. The foreman of the jury in Mum's original trial phoned into a BBC Radio 5 Live programme and told listeners that, having heard all the facts about Mum's life, none of which had been revealed in the trial, he was now doubtful about her conviction. He followed up his phone call by writing to Jack Straw. I was so moved by his intervention that I gave a quote to the local Bradford paper, the *Telegraph & Argus*: 'It's big of him to come out and say this after so long. He's a bit of a hero.'

Inevitably, Imy, Foz and I added our own letters to the growing pile on Jack Straw's desk. I hope the short extracts below illustrate our heartfelt desire to see our Mum outside the prison gates once more. More than any memory of mine, they show just how painful Mum's imprisonment was for us all.

'My mother is in prison for killing a man who used to abuse her', wrote Foz. 'When she was found guilty of murder, it was like being stabbed ten times over; even now, writing this letter, I have tears pouring down my face. I was away in Pakistan when my aunt told me the news that my mum had been imprisoned for murder. I was crying so loudly the people next door came running to our house to find out what happened. I stopped going to school, I just wanted to see my mum. A month later I returned home to the UK. I can't tell you the feeling I had when I eventually saw her again. She could not stop looking at me. She was so thin. The last six years have been horrible but knowing now what she suffered is even worse . . . Mr Straw, I'd like you to look at this case and reduce my mother's sentence. We can't cope any more, we need to be a family again. I just want to be happy and that means being with my mum.'

Imy got straight to the heart of the matter: 'My heart was broken knowing what my mother went through. She suffered a lot and still is today. Yet she didn't give any hint about what she was going through . . . I don't blame her for killing him, honestly. I didn't want to say this, but Mr Straw, if I'd known, I'd probably be sat in a prison now, locked up for murder . . . She's not the cold-blooded killer some people think she is, she's just a sweet mother who tried doing the best for her kids. I love her with all my heart . . . I hope you can help put that happiness back into our lives.'

'I am writing to support my mum's application for a review of tariff', my own letter began. 'I appreciate that you will be presented with lots of professional opinions about my mother's background and character; however, I don't think any of them will be able to portray her as the mother I'd like you to understand her as . . . There are, in my view, countless reasons why my mother's sentence should be reduced. If I was to make a list, at the top would be, "She's suffered enough." I don't believe that the prison service is serving its purpose by keeping Mum behind bars. The simple reason being that she understands that what she did was wrong and does not need reforming into a law-abiding citizen . . . For more than six years I have tried my best to be a good parent to my siblings, Amrahz and Fozia. It hasn't been easy, especially when I compare myself to my mother . . . I didn't have a clue how to run a home but I learnt the ropes, it took time but I got there . . . Mr Straw, we were in effect vulnerable youngsters, we could have well been part of government statistics of offenders, drug users, young single mothers and many more. Thankfully we're not, and that's all down to our mother. The love and respect we have for each other and others is because, despite everything, she did a damn good job of bringing us up. If it wasn't for my mother's love and guidance, I could never have kept this family together . . . Mr Straw, I am begging for compassion and understanding from you. We just want to be a family again.'

More than anything, those letters take me back to the years the three of us clung to each other while Mum sat alone behind bars.

Today, I can say that I am grateful for our experiences, that I am proud of the strong, independent individuals we became. While some might believe that we should leave the past behind, that we have to keep looking forward, I'm not sure I buy into this. Isn't it our pasts that define the strength we need to develop to face the future? If we let go of our past experiences, we are denying the journey, the wealth of experience gathered along the way to help us reach our destination.

I don't deny my adversity, and I don't hold on to my past for the pain but for the lessons.

In November 1999, as we were drawing closer to presenting our final submissions to Jack Straw's office, I learnt that I was to be one of the first recipients of the Emma Humphreys Memorial Prize. This annual award had been set up by the campaigning group Justice for Women, who had been involved in Mum's appeal. It was established to honour the memory of Emma Humphreys who, having been drawn into drugs and prostitution, killed her violent pimp in 1985. She successfully appealed her conviction at the Court of Appeal in 1995, arguing provocation. Sadly, she died of an accidental overdose of prescribed medication in 1998.

Justice for Women said, 'Although Emma is no longer here to enjoy the benefits of her court victory, she exemplifies the fighting spirit of women. It is appropriate that this is her prize because, against all odds, she fought for herself and other women. Similarly, Naseem fights not just for her mother and for other women, but against bigotry. Like Emma, she has great strength in the most difficult of times.'

It was a huge honour to win the award and it marked a watershed moment in terms of my own development as a campaigner. I'd been recognised by some of the powerful women I had admired for so long. In my acceptance speech, where I made one more plea to the Home Secretary, I drew the connection between the personal and the political: 'A decent reduction will mean everything to us. This isn't hollow rhetoric, not just a bit of campaigning now and again. This is about a life destroyed, a family destroyed. The campaign represents a struggle against the sexual and economic exploitation of many Asian women.'

It was around this time that I was to visit Parliament for the first time. Our local MP, Marsha Singh, invited me to Westminster so that I could present our petition in person. I walk past that office a lot these days, but back then, the only thing that I remember of the visit was that Jack Straw was a lot shorter than I anticipated and the coffee was horrendous.

The three years I'd spent as the figurehead of the campaign developed and launched by Southall Black Sisters had turned me from a streetwise but naive kid into someone who could understand strategy, planning and future forecasting. It was a big change which I probably didn't fully appreciate at the time, as all my attention was focused on securing an early release for Mum.

Nothing mattered more than that.

13

A Suitable Boy

In many ways, my journey to Westminster began with Southall Black Sisters and the campaign to secure Mum's release from prison. It had never crossed my mind that a parliamentary career might be a possible outcome of the years I had spent campaigning and protesting, but today I recognise how the fusing of the personal and the political ignited something vital inside of me, and the emotional culmination of my life's experiences coalesced into a path. But I would have plenty more to learn and to absorb before I'd be in any way ready for a life in politics.

I moved jobs once again and was now working as an outreach worker for the Asian Disability Network, the Bradford-based organisation that supports women with disabilities which later became known as BradNet. Now, I had the opportunity to help these women gain access to the services and benefits they were entitled to. This was positive, proactive work, which brought about real and immediate change in the lives of women and children and gave me an informed insight into how disability can affect life choices.

I pursued each case with an ever-increasing sense of urgency, which, in reality, was partly fuelled by my own increasing sense of injustice as it became clear to me just how little support Imy, Foz and I had received during the years of Mum's incarceration. But facing adversity had its benefits too. Having to support myself and my siblings, running Mum's appeal campaign, and facing the seemingly never-ending hostility from my community – it put a fire in my belly. And so I was doubly motivated to make sure that the vulnerable people I was tasked with supporting received everything they were entitled to. There is a knock-on effect if people don't take up the support and services which are available – it shows up later in ill health for both the disabled and carers alike. I felt like I was making a difference to people's lives and flourished in my work, as a result of which I was profiled at a national level in the NHS and used as a case study to recruit more people into the social care profession.

The year 2000 was significant in several ways. First and foremost, in the two years since Mum's appeal had failed, we'd spent our time lobbying the Home Secretary to reduce her tariff and finally – finally! – it paid off. The lobbying was hard work because of the sheer force of our determination to maintain our earlier momentum. In whatever spare time I could conjure up, I was on the road, speaking at events up and down the country, organising petitions and encouraging as many people as possible to appeal to Jack Straw. Southall Black Sisters lent their support every step of the way.

While Foz was very much involved, travelling with me to campaign events, Imy didn't want to be in the headlights of the campaign – talking about Mum's sexual abuse was still deeply uncomfortable for him.

But for first time since we had begun campaigning, it felt

like someone with the power to make a difference had really heard us. The Home Secretary announced that he had taken into consideration all the evidence submitted to him and decided that he would reduce Mum's original sentence from twenty years to twelve.

I wouldn't say that we celebrated the news. Mum still had to serve four more years before she could come home. By this point, she had been in inside for a total of eight years, and she was diminished by the time she'd spent away from her family. Even so, Mum was heartened to receive the recognition at last that her case deserved some kind of reappraisal.

The press came out in force – this was big news and the public campaign had been vindicated. But once again, our extended family didn't reach out to acknowledge the victory, despite the Lord Chief Justice's statement that there was no doubt that Mum had been driven to kill. She was now a believable woman where in the past there had been zero empathy for her case. Even though I'd have liked Mr Straw to reduce the tariff further still, we were grateful for that recognition.

I vowed to continue campaigning as publicly and as visibly as I could on Mum's behalf, and on the behalf of other abused women. If her case could help bring about a more enlightened judicial approach to vulnerable women, then it was important to keep using her example. And of course, who knew, if we kept Mum's name in the news, there might be a miracle and her freedom brought forward.

It was during 2000 that the pressures I'd been under for so long began to take their toll. I became keenly aware that I was not feeling as resilient as usual.

The week before I went for my interview with BradNet, the Asian Disability Network, I experienced a serious mental health collapse. One day I started crying and couldn't stop. The upheaval of the last two years had finally brought me to breaking point. In utter despair, my tears flowed and flowed.

While my world felt like it was caving in, I was lucid enough to recognise that I needed help. I wasn't suicidal, but it was clear that I was spiralling into depression and an intervention was needed. After three days of tears, a brilliant community psychiatric nurse from the home treatment service, Salma Yasmin, was sent to my house. This was the first time I opened up about all the pressures I had been under. It was a relief to talk so frankly to a professional after all this time. While fronting Mum's campaign with Southall Black Sisters and Justice for Women, I had no choice but to be the strong one – to be bold and positive throughout. During those busy years, there hadn't been any time or space in which I could show a glimmer of weakness or take a step back. While I don't regret it for a minute, inevitably the pressure to keep going, to keep fighting, built and built inside me.

After we talked, I told Salma that I didn't want to be admitted to hospital. It was too important for me to get that job at BradNet. I parked my emotions, went for the interview and nailed it.

I learnt that I have the ability to put whatever is going on in my life to one side and be ruthlessly pragmatic when I need to be. It would be fair to say that these days, when the hill becomes steeper, I increase my speed – very little will slow me down when I know I'm on the right path.

*

While I understood that my mental health was suffering, I was relieved I wasn't suicidal. As much as I was ambitious in my career, I was even more ambitious to overcome my despair. I didn't turn to my siblings for support, because I still maintained my maternal role within our family. How could I break down in front of them? What would it do to *them*? There was no way I was going to introduce more pain and more anxiety into their lives.

But maybe this was a bad idea. Maybe if I had shown them just how vulnerable I was in that moment, they would have understood that none of us is invincible – not even me. It might, in turn, have made them even more resilient. But if I'm completely honest, they both have powerful coping mechanisms – they don't really need to be quite as tough as me. It's one thing to be hardy, but too much self-reliance comes with a cost, and that's mental wellbeing. I don't wish that on my children or my siblings.

Today, now that I'm older and wiser, I can recognise the signs of impending collapse and am much more attuned to those periods where my foot doesn't need to press quite so hard on the pedal. From the moment Mum was arrested, I had been expected to show no weakness, no vulnerability, to be the rock for those who needed me. I had survived my marriage, my mother being accused and found guilty of murder, and campaigning for years and years for her release, as well as taking care of my siblings. I can see why others might look at me and think that I was in control of our lives and coping magnificently with everything that was being thrown our way. It never occurred to anyone that I was in any way struggling at the time, and this was because I didn't want them to know. But I had never once stopped to consider my own vulnerability. I was far too busy to ponder the price of my boundless energy or my laser-sharp focus on the goal of Mum's release. There was always too much to do. Beyond a few nights a month, where I lost myself to the beats in a downtown nightclub, I had little time off.

In psychological terms, as I would discover later on in my career when I moved into leadership roles in the NHS, I am a total extravert: I live my life through engagement with others, I tend not to pause and reflect on how I might feel. I am 100 per cent action.

Did I stop to consider my two previous suicide attempts? No, in my mind, they were merely accidents, odd flashes of weakness after which I picked myself up and re-entered the fray. But it was by talking to that psychiatric nurse in 2000 that I first made the connection between the emotional turmoil rumbling away inside, and what I projected from the surface. I was finally able to begin the process of keeping an eye on myself. No one had ever really kept an eye on me apart from Mum, and she'd been absent for the last eight years.

Trauma begets trauma and the other big trigger for me around this time was to do with my father. We didn't have much contact during my years of campaigning for Mum and Imy, Foz and I still had a troubled relationship with him. We had never really reconciled after his most recent disowning of me when I ended it once and for all with Mazhar.

Dad's health was deteriorating and when he was given a terminal cancer diagnosis in 2001, it knocked me for six. Perhaps understandably, my reaction took me entirely by surprise. I wasn't aware of any deep feelings of love for my father – he had been a brute to my mother and had left his young family to fight for survival while he went on the run with the sixteen-year-old neighbour – so why was I suddenly so upset?

Once again, I credit Salma Yasmin as my mental health champion. My exchanges with her around this time helped me to understand that my tears were not an expression of grief or compassion for Dad's impending death. They were tears of rage. While I cried and manically cleaned my house, I began to process my anger. Dad had never once over the years acknowledged his share of responsibility for all that had happened in his children's lives, in his wife's life. And now he was dying his way out of it.

'It's OK to be angry, Naz,' Salma told me. 'And it's OK to be angry with your dad. You're not shaming anyone, you're not being unfair; it's just what it is. So accept it, think about it and work through it.'

This was the first time in my life that I had been told my rage was legitimate. That it was OK not to feel OK. The legacy of shame, of guilt, of thwarted izzat – I carried it all inside me, buried like some sick secret. I hadn't been raised to vocalise my feelings or express my concerns. While my resilience knew no bounds, something else had been eaten away by endless disappointment, endless demands to behave in a certain way, to be obedient. I realised that once these codes of honour and good behaviour were stripped away, I was unaware of my own likes and dislikes. Who was I really? I had never been encouraged to be the best I could be, to go after my dreams. I wasn't even allowed a fringe or a pair of trousers without having to fight for them. I had to marry at fifteen years old. And all because I didn't have a *dad*. And why was *he* such a prize? This man who had shed his responsibilities and left us vulnerable, impoverished and dishonoured.

No wonder I was angry. But owning my fury, acknowledging it and expressing it, was like drawing back heavy curtains to reveal a sunny day. Not only were my feelings legitimate, but they were also vindicated. I felt like I suddenly had permission to acknowledge that my resentment wasn't unreasonable. And it was utterly liberating. I could physically feel the weight of guilt and expectation lifting away.

Imy, Foz and I had an awkward relationship with our dad. Whenever he was with his new wife and their children, he behaved as though he was ashamed of us. If we were ever invited to a family event (and it happened rarely enough), he remained distant, almost unfriendly. When he was on his own, however, he tried to make a bit more of an effort by asking us how we were – giving the appearance, at least, of a caring father. He was our dad and we wanted to feel a sense of family, so we looked forward to those few and far between occasions when we were allowed into his life. He made it hard, though. One thing I remember – it's always the small things, isn't it? – was the time Foz gave him some comfortable Clarks sandals to wear around the house, because his mobility was declining. He wouldn't wear those damn sandals when his new family was around, because they were a gift from the wrong family member. That really hurt. Foz had been denied by my father before she was ever born, and here he was, doing it again, and again. With each abandonment of his children, he doubled down on his paternal failings.

Of the three of us, because I was five years older than Imy, I had more vivid memories of living with Dad. I was his brown girl in the ring after all, and I could clearly recall being loved by him as a child. At the same time, I had equally powerful memories of him dragging Mum across the floor by her hair, and of his indifference if Mum was ever physically assaulted by a member of his extended family.

Once I discovered that Dad's cancer was terminal, these memories and the events of the previous couple of decades welled up inside me and I felt, very strongly, that I wanted some answers from him. If I wasn't going to attempt closure now, then when? Why had he left us all those years ago? Didn't he feel sorry? Wasn't he ashamed for the dishonour he had heaped upon us? Wasn't he regretful for how our lives had turned out as a result of his abandonment? How could he stand watching his children move from one cramped and cold house to another? Couldn't he now, knowing he didn't have much time left, talk to me?

It seemed he couldn't. Or wouldn't.

I didn't overstep any boundaries or put any pressure on him – he was my father, and in my mind that meant he was still deserving of respect – and I was mindful that he was now very ill. But I gave him the opportunity to reflect on the past and discuss his role, or lack of it, in our lives.

It was as though I was talking to him in Spanish. He didn't appear to think that he had done anything wrong. Entirely oblivious to the pain he had caused, the same tired sentence poured out of his mouth: 'I really tried with your mother, I really did.' I'll never know what this 'trying' looked like, because he never explained himself. My mum had been a loyal wife and in return he had savagely beat her.

Two years later, the cancer killed him.

Now, more than twenty-two years on, I can honestly say that I feel nothing for my father. Where there might be grief, there's a numbness, a void of emotion. The expression of my rage was like a blood-letting; the resentment and pain dissolving just like his presence in our lives.

And guess what, the world moved on.

This period of emotional upheaval was memorable for something else too: I got myself a fella. As you can imagine, what with the combination of my scarring experience with Mazhar and our subsequent divorce, and the intensity of the campaign for Mum's release – so much of which was focused on male brutality towards women – I hadn't really imagined that I was in the market for romance. I hadn't consciously turned my back on the idea, or on men in general – it just didn't seem a very likely turn of events. But then, facilitated by a mutual friend, I met Lee on a blind date. I wasn't in any dating scene; that wasn't for me. If I was going to meet a man, it was with the intention of finding a life partner, someone to settle down with and marry, just like Foz had done.

Lee was different. For a start, he wasn't from our original Pakistani community. He was a Pathan of Afghani heritage, whose family came from the Swat Valley. Lee was a Westernised, laid-back kind of guy. We didn't share the same cultural reference points and we spoke different languages, he Pashtu and me Urdu and Punjabi, but that didn't matter one jot.

He was what I'd term a liberal Muslim – a true believer, like me, abiding by the rules of Islam. While neither of us was what you might call a practising Muslim, we were very secure in our identity. Lee had a modern, contemporary outlook on the world. There was no question of me covering my head or dressing in a certain way – on the contrary, he loved going out dancing as much as I did. Lee was good-looking (it helps!) and he liked music, used to be DJ in fact, and played the kind of soul, hip hop and dance music that I loved. His family was also part of the Syed line of Muslim families, and as I've described, those cultural affiliations still ran deep inside me.

I'd had to support Foz through her engagement and marriage to Pav. Pav wasn't a Syed, and when Foz announced she was going to marry him, I received a stream of outraged calls from family members telling me that I needed to dissuade her, that it was completely wrong for a Shah woman to marry outside the Syed bloodline. They made their views very clear to Foz, too, telling her she was in danger – threats of violence came easily in those days. If she had proclaimed she wanted to marry an Englishman, she might have faced less vitriol. We have a relative who still suffers the shame of marrying a non-Syed to this day.

When one of my uncles told me that Foz was bringing fresh shame on the family, I explained to him: 'Uncle, as far as I'm concerned, there is no hierarchy among Muslims. Maybe there are those who are more pious and observant, but the last sermon of the Prophet, peace be upon him, stated that we are all equal. When you go to Hajj, you all shave your heads, and you all circle the Ka'aba in the middle of the Grand Mosque in Mecca, seven times. Can you tell who's a Syed and who isn't? In the house of God, if He doesn't discriminate, how can you?'

Foz, however, remained resolute throughout. I supported her completely and told our interfering family members that they should do the same. My sister didn't have to run away with Pav because she had her siblings' support. And Foz has proved, with her successful marriage and loving family, that she made the right choice for her life.

But while it may not be easy for everyone to understand, I do get it. I get that we Syeds have a responsibility to behave better than our neighbours, to honour our lineage, to lead by example. This is the pressure of ancestry. Even today, someone or other will tell me I'm only doing what's expected of me because I'm a Syed – nothing more. But I can't square that line of thinking. I know I'm not better than anyone else because of the circumstance of my birth.

It is the patriarchal mindset, manipulating Islam in order to control women rather than empower them. I respect the community aspect of our culture, where family is celebrated – after all, family is at the centre of Islam, and if you have strong family roots, you'll raise strong, pious individuals. But within the culture I was raised in, you are the keeper and propagator of this box of izzat, and if you misbehave, you risk your honour and the honour of your whole family. The agency I had in my community was defined by izzat, by honour and shame. While izzat might drive you to succeed, it also oppresses you. The trick is finding the right balance.

For me, the balance came with my spiritual evolution, which began when I started working at BradNet, through my then manager, Mohammed Shabbir. I had obviously worked with Muslim men before but, at the NHS, I was now working alongside men like Shabbir who had professional qualifications and successful careers. He stopped me in my tracks one day, did Shabbir: he'd come to our house for dinner and, while I was making the food, the stereo was playing hip hop. Shabbir came over to me, very politely:

'Naz, can you change that Tupac music, please?'

'Why, don't you like hip hop?' I asked him, thinking maybe it was just a bit too fashionable for my serious colleague.

'It's not that,' he said. 'It's the lyrics. They're massively disrespectful towards women. Don't you hear that too?'

Of course, he was right. I just hadn't considered it before. I was amazed, after all my experience working alongside black and white feminists, that it took a brown man to point out to me the deeply misogynistic lyrics. Shabbir is one of a kind: thoughtful, cultured, loyal. He is a very important person to me still, and his daughter now works for me in my constituency office.

As my faith developed, Islam gave me the permission to see through the cultural strictures that hold women back. I have realised that viewing Islam through the lens of patriarchy is only ever going to give you a patriarchal, oppressive and sexist system.

But at the same time, I can't deny that the deeply ingrained cultural beliefs I had grown up with were, at some level, satisfied by the fact that Lee was a Syed. Go figure.

Today, there is much more tolerance for marrying outside the lineage, but Foz's case was unprecedented. Maybe we can credit her for paving the way forward.

Lee and I moved into a rented bungalow in Sand Piper Mews

in Bradford in 2000. We didn't marry straightaway; instead, we decided to live together, neither of us giving much thought to the cultural 'rules' of propriety. But I couldn't tell Mum I had shacked up with a guy outside of marriage – she would have been scandalised.

A couple of years later, Lee and I did marry and together we bought a house in Daisy Hill Lane. In 2003, I became pregnant with my daughter, Leyana.

Lee was the first man I can say that I had a mutually respectful relationship with. He cared for me, and I cared for him. There was genuine affection there – the opposite of my first experience of marriage. Lee allowed me to be myself during my depressive episodes, supporting me by allowing me to simply be me. He gave me the hug I needed when I needed it. But since I was still struggling to find my identity, I found it difficult to rely on someone else. It's that old cliché – you can't allow someone else to be there for you unless you're there for yourself. I wasn't quite there yet.

For the first time in my life, I was in what I would consider a normal relationship. Lee didn't care that Mum was in prison. He didn't judge me – nor did he judge her. I didn't have to justify my family. He saw me for me, not for the sum of my baggage.

Even though I was on the outer edges of my community, outside the remit of its structures, I was still proud I had found another Syed. I was proud that maybe this time I would escape judgement and derision.

To a large extent I was still conditioned enough by my culture to try to be a good girl.

14

Freedom, at Last

My three years at BradNet were significant for me. They took me out of the realm of domestic abuse and into an entirely different territory, where Asian women with disabilities and children faced daily struggles which were invisible to most able-bodied citizens. How to manage a home, how to shop, how to adapt to work and transport, how to claim the benefits that might make life just that little bit more tolerable – these were all genuinely satisfying areas in which to make a difference, and it did feel like I was improving lives.

In 2003, however, an opportunity came up which I couldn't turn down: the chance to move into the broad arena of NHS management as Patient and Public Involvement Co-ordinator for the NHS in Bradford.

The five years I was to spend in the NHS truly prepared me for what was to come when the world of politics came knocking. I received a real understanding of how systems succeed or fail for ordinary people. I learnt how decisions taken centrally actually impact people on the ground, a great guide to what was to follow within Westminster. And crucially, I was introduced to the theory and practice of leadership, the word I use perhaps more than any other in my political life today and which, if I had my way, would be the litmus test by which we judge the suitability of all future politicians.

The NHS may have many problems, but what's often overlooked is the way in which decision-making flows through. It has much less of a top-down trajectory than our mainstream political system, because the decisions – often political ones – which are made about the NHS are systematically filtered through a management system that is inextricably linked to operations. Senior NHS managers are very tied into operational delivery in a way that politicians today are often not. When a politician announces a benefits change or an alteration to asylum procedures or a new law relating to security on the streets, that politician very rarely sees with his or her own eyes the impact of their decision upon the populace. I was to spend the next five years steeping myself in the application of process and how that is felt by those on the receiving end.

When I began working for the NHS in 2003, I had an annual budget of just under half a million pounds to allocate. Five years later, once I had reached the level of Commissioning Manager for Public Health in the district, I was overseeing a budget of £5.2 million. By this time, I was working closely with colleagues in London who were issuing new directives and edicts from the Department of Health, and it was my job to work within those at a local level. For the first time, I was able to witness with my own eyes how national politics – whether Labour or Tory led – impacted society, because I had to make a limited budget work as effectively as possible for all citizens and still adhere to the central government guidelines.

It was stimulating work, which fostered fascinating

discussions and arguments among my colleagues and the people we served. I didn't really stop to reflect on how my campaigning work had opened up such a satisfying career path for me. I didn't have the time to reflect. I felt a great pressure to work, to support myself, to gain some security after years of poverty. That I could afford to help my siblings, buy a nice car and enjoy a weekend away was a revelation.

I measured my worth against graduates of the day. If a graduate was earning £30,000 per year, then that's what I was aiming for. I was filled with ambition in those days, caught up with being the best that I could be. It wasn't until 2008, when I took part in a leadership development programme, that everything began to fall into place. I fell in love with the concept of leadership and for the first time I had a context for my ambition: I now had the theory and an understanding of my conditioning. It was fascinating to learn why I behaved the way I did. I understood that for much of my life I had been lurching from one disaster to another – or following blind ambition. Finally, I was developing a skillset that I could use to face any challenges I encountered, whether in my personal life or in my career. I was beginning to learn that the more crises I faced, the better I became at coping. Most people, when chaos enters their lives, see other areas – like work – begin to suffer. But I discovered that the more drama came my way, the more I tended to excel elsewhere.

And my resilience in the face of crisis felt like a superpower.

I was so immersed in the need to both continue campaigning to highlight Mum's plight and the plight of women like her, and to fight against the daily discrimination she faced inside

FREEDOM, AT LAST

prison from an uncaring system, that I don't think I was aware of how comprehensively it consumed my life.

The one time I had a glimpse of how I might appear to other people was when I first moved from BradNet to the NHS. I was very passionate and highly articulate about wanting to make sure that vulnerable people received the level of care within the health service they deserved – I was so focused on this, I may have appeared a little obsessed. Ali Jan Haider, my friend and mentor, once asked me: 'How much of this is about you?' That gave me a jolt, because of course he was right. The injustice Mum had suffered was a constant flame, fuelling my drive every single day, in every part of my life. This is just as true today as it was then.

As the years passed and the date for Mum's early release drew closer, we'd face one further indignity. Even though her sentence had been cut, the system remained unequal, and prejudice towards Mum and her particular cultural experiences prevailed.

The purpose of prison is three-fold: punishment, repentance and rehabilitation. Parole boards also have to satisfy themselves that inmates are remorseful. During the four years since Mum's sentence had been reviewed, she had made numerous applications for parole. She was required to convince the powers that be that she was no longer a risk, and that she had understood and had repented for her crime.

In Mum's case, her repentance model was namaz – or prayer. Mum's language around the issue of repentance was culturally specific. Rather than explaining to the parole board how sorry she was for her crimes, she turned to God for forgiveness. She explained to God the reasons why she was driven to such drastic measures and asked Him for His mercy. However, the Eurocentric model of repentance and rehabilitation didn't allow for this kind of nuanced approach and the board turned down her application for parole numerous times.

It wasn't until Southall Black Sisters stepped in and hired a transcultural psychologist to give cultural context to Mum's repentance model and explain Mum's mental state due to her cultural conditioning that the parole board accepted she wasn't a risk, that she had repented and been sufficiently punished.

Mum ended up serving two years longer than her reduced tariff because of a cultural misunderstanding.

Eventually, in 2006, I was told by her parole officer that Mum would be allowed to leave prison on day release, to spend some time with us and return to the prison at night. Once she had demonstrated that she could manage these days out, her time behind bars would come to an end and she would finally be free to leave for good.

We were informed that Bradford was out of bounds initially, but she could stay on its outskirts.

'Why?' I asked. 'Bradford is where we all live; it's where we've been preparing for her homecoming all these years.'

The reason was because the victim's family lived in Bradford, and naturally it would be upsetting for Mum to appear among them out of the blue.

I understood the argument but by this point we just wanted our mum home.

For the first few day releases, we had to meet Mum at Foz's mother-in-law's house, which was sufficiently far enough away from the city centre to satisfy the parole board. But it meant

FREEDOM, AT LAST

that Mum couldn't come and visit the homes of her three children, now settled with families of their own. My daughter, Leyana, was three years old at the time. These were, of course, emotional days filled with tears; we spent most of them just hugging each other, looking at one another and celebrating the fact we were together once more.

It was quite shocking to see how weak and fragile she seemed outside the prison environment, but my mum is a brave woman. She had survived fourteen years in prison and was just fifty-four years old.

Mum was timid at first, hollowed out, nervous like a tiny shivering bird. To some extent, she's still like that today – nobody could go through what she's been through without being, in some profound way, broken by it all. But she was out. She was finally free. And once the probation board was satisfied that this woman might be allowed to roam the streets of Bradford, she returned to the city.

On her first real day of freedom, I picked Mum up from the prison and took her directly to my house, where Foz, Imy and Pav were waiting on the doorstep. We got through the front door and into the hallway, but we never made it to the living room – we were in bits. As we stood hugging and crying, the weight of all those lost and painful years was finally finding its own release. We wept for the time we had been apart, for the struggles we had endured to bring us to this moment. This tiny woman – so small, yet such a huge part of what made us the people we became. I could feel her bones beneath her coat. She was so physically insubstantial; a breath of wind might have carried her away. But she was happy, reunited with her children, her grandchildren.

We were a family once more and I was never letting her go again.

Eventually, we sat down to a feast prepared by Foz. After a few minutes of staring at her food, Mum caught my eye.

'Could I use the toilet?' she asked, breaking my heart.

'Oh, Mum, you don't need to ask permission. Nobody's gonna stop you doing anything or going wherever you want ever again.'

I might have been surprised by her question, but what did we expect after fourteen years inside? Mum was institutionalised, and it would take some time to break the habits of her incarceration.

The rules of prison life had been deeply ingrained and, even today, they continue to define her behaviour. Mum absolutely hates being cooped up indoors, even though she's riddled with arthritis and has had knee replacements and continues to receive steroid injections to help with the pain – pain so severe that there are days she struggles to get out of bed. She is in her seventies now but come hell or high water, she will leave the house. She will suffer any discomfort to be outside in the fresh air.

While she was in prison, Mum carried out a work placement in a charity shop in York. Her love of charity shops has never left her; she's always on the lookout for a bargain. Nothing makes her happier than trawling the Oxfams of Bradford; and she adores the London charity shops, which, she claims, offer a better class of bargain.

Mum could have secured a council house when she was released from prison, but she refused. Her desire to have her own home has never left her. It remains a part of her izzat.

FREEDOM, AT LAST

She believes that if she's renting privately or owns her own home, it's a sign that she's doing well; she's not relying on the state for her welfare. But more significantly, she's showing the community that she's coping just fine on her own, despite their lack of support over the years. These days she lives in a granny flat within my brother's sizeable home and loves to entertain. She takes enormous pride in her space.

Gradually, Mum reintegrated herself into the community. During the turbulent fourteen years she had been away, we had made some inroads. Foz and I were married, working women – and respectable to boot. But while there were some who would have nothing to do with us or my mum, her family in Pakistan had never severed ties. She had kept in touch with them during her entire incarceration, the same family who had prayed for the curse that had landed her in prison to be lifted. I guess it worked, eventually.

Mum was never prouder of me than in those days following her release. Proud of all of us for campaigning so hard, for the fact that we never wavered in our visits. That we believed, wholeheartedly, that she would come home to us. She was grateful, knowing she might still be inside if it wasn't for our efforts.

She knew, only too well, that if she had never disclosed the facts about her abuse, she would have served a further six years in prison. My mum had been bullied and beaten her whole life – first by her husband and his family, then through the sexual exploitation she suffered at the hands of Azam. That she was imprisoned at all is almost unthinkable.

These men cared nothing that she was a mother, that she worked hard to feed and clothe her children. They cared nothing for her piety or her honour. She existed only to fulfil their pathological desire to dominate and crush another human being.

When we lose our sense of decency and our obligation to nurture and support our peers, we might as well be animals scrabbling round the undergrowth, using our strength and cunning to take what isn't ours and subjugate the weak.

My anger and grief about what happened to my mum have never abated.

Even though she'd been away from us for fourteen long years, stuck behind bars in Durham, New Hall, Foston Hall, Askham Grange and Holloway, Mum had been a constant, daily presence for me and my siblings. During those long years, I never considered taking a holiday or being anywhere where she wasn't able to reach out to me.

Finally, with Mum home, I had more time and energy to devote to my career within the NHS. For the first time, I had a bit of space to myself and my life was about to change – again.

15

Mouse on a Treadmill

As 2008 drew to a close, I completed a transformational leadership programme – a national training initiative geared towards building a new generation of Black, Asian and minority ethnic health service leaders.

Only twenty-four people a year were selected to go on the four-month course. I told my interviewer that I could sometimes come across as blunt and intimidating, and that I needed a little more self-awareness if I was to become an effective and compassionate leader.

Course completed, I was brimming with enthusiasm and ideas, excited about how I might use this new knowledge to make sense of the world around me. Everything that I'd learnt so far while campaigning for Mum, working as a disability advocate or managing services in the NHS now made sense within a clear framework of leadership.

But before I had much of an opportunity to put this new understanding into practice, I discovered that I was going to need to fall back on an earlier lesson to manage an emerging crisis. I was going to have to rely once more on my old friend, resilience.

In 2009, I moved from my NHS post to a new local government programme, Get Connected – an initiative set up to tackle post-9/11 terrorism and weaken radicalisation. I saw it as a way to use my new-found skills and commission a whole new leadership programme for Muslim women in the region. I was inspired by the opportunity.

Within just two weeks of taking up my new role, I became aware of problems in this organisation that were obvious to me, having worked in a position where I was responsible for commissioning over £5 million of projects a year. I immediately raised a concern and insisted from this point forward every claim had to be put into writing. I was a brown woman whose mother had been in prison, and I'd learnt the hard way that I always needed to be squeaky clean when it came to anything to do with public finances.

I went to see my boss, who assured me that structures would be tightened up. But my boss was also my consultant and chair of my board – three roles in one. How could I raise an issue with my manager about my consultant when they were one and the same person? It was a clear conflict of interest. Coming out of my campaigning years, I had a heightened sense of injustice and criminality.

I then discovered that the entire leadership programme, which I believed I'd been tasked with initiating, overseeing and implementing, had already been commissioned out to an organisation by someone else. In other words, I wasn't part of the commissioning team, I wasn't a part of the programme's development, and it wasn't going to be my baby.

I was incensed by this revelation. The stress from the endless confrontations made me ill. I had worked hard to build my career, progressing from a local to a regional role, but as the new kid on the block, I feared I would be scapegoated when the mismanagement of public funds came to light.

I wasn't having it.

No action was taken to address what were, to me, obvious financial irregularities within the organisation – but I wasn't surprised. Eventually, I had no choice but to become a whistleblower. I lodged a formal complaint with my manager's manager, but instead of answering my questions, they just dug themselves deeper into a hole.

So, after making the complaint, I was put on gardening leave in January 2010 while the situation was investigated.

And because I could see that it was a clear-cut, black-and-white case, I took them to a tribunal.

The timing was far from ideal. I had had another baby by this point, a son, Aydan, and was pregnant with my third. The stress was mounting, and cracks began to appear in my relationship with Lee.

My union refused to offer financial support, believing I had no chance of winning. Every barrister I consulted said the same. Without union backing, I couldn't afford to hire legal representation, so I decided to represent myself.

Day after day, I studied employment tribunals and pored over case law relevant to my grievance – focusing on the judgments that set legal precedent. I needed to ensure my arguments were watertight. I knew they were. I just had to hang on and block out the so-called expert advice.

The 2008 recession had devastated the job market. There was no going back to the NHS, and I had been made redundant. So there I was – two years on, having lost a senior public sector role due to whistle-blowing, with a mother who'd spent fourteen years in jail, and a brown face. That was not the easiest CV for re-entering professional employment. I was out of a job and desperately needed to earn. I looked around but there just wasn't anything suitable on offer. Which is why I ploughed my redundancy settlement into Monster Fun, a play centre I launched with Imy and Lee.

Never one to stand still, even I was amazed at how much I was piling onto my plate. I was taking local government to a tribunal while I was pregnant. I was working all hours of the day to get the play centre up and running, and spending the evenings studying case law and arguing with Lee.

But while none of it was ideal, I cracked on and it paid off. I won the case and some compensation, even though all I had wanted was an apology and an admission that my concerns were legitimate.

Those days were strange and difficult. The tribunal had put a huge strain on my marriage. In the past, I'd been out at work all day, engaging in satisfying, high-level commissioning for the NHS. When I returned home, I was free to play the perfect wife. Now, Lee and I were under financial pressure and we were in each other's space all day long – at work, with the play centre and at home, raising our children.

Lee and I enjoyed a very traditional home life. Although we loved our music and dancing – and in some of the more pious sections of the Muslim community that's not hugely approved of – in other ways, we couldn't have been a more conservative couple. I managed all the cooking and cleaning. If we visited friends for supper and Lee complimented our hostess on one of the dishes she had prepared, I'd go out of my way to find the recipe and try to replicate it for him at home. If the football was on, I'd tell Lee to put his feet up and I'd tiptoe around the kitchen, preparing snacks while he and his pals yelled at the TV. I was proud of our house; I liked having friends over so I could cook for them and show off our new three-piece suite. While I was earning good money during our marriage so was Lee, and we enjoyed our new cars in the driveway. I even got the mosaic bathroom I had so admired back at Rahila Gupta's house when we started campaigning for Mum's appeal.

I have beautiful memories of that period of my life. For the first time in a relationship, I had dared to dream. While our marriage ultimately didn't survive – we parted in August 2010 – today, Lee lives just around the corner from me and the kids and continues to be a wonderful father. We remain good friends to this day.

It does make me chuckle now, looking back at that proud little housewife, scrubbing her kitchen worktops until they gleamed. I know where it all comes from – it comes from Mum's determination to provide us with a decent family home. In her eyes, and in the eyes of most Pakistani women, the absolute cast-iron rule is that you must always offer hospitality to your husband and to your guests. And I'd be lying if I said I don't adore playing the host. If you turned up at my house today, my training would immediately kick in and I would offer you a drink, ask you if you were hungry and I'd probably insist on serving one of my homemade chapatis or parathas together with some chicken or lamb curry, which will be in the fridge or freezer just waiting for someone like you to appear. I can't do anything else – it's a habit that will stay with me until I die. The woman of the house will never allow you to walk away from her home hungry or thirsty.

Of course, I call myself a feminist and I can see how my mindset might seem at odds to that of some of my sisters. Why couldn't Lee make *me* supper? Why do you have to offer me food if I come to your house – why can't you ask me to bring a takeaway? Well, because that's not how it works for me. Hospitality runs in my blood. It's this awareness that helps me better understand how women like my mum can end up in situations of such peril. Being of service is a powerful cultural instinct which is passed down from generation to generation, and I'm not going to stand up and say it's wrong. It's part of my life and part of my Muslim heritage of which I am deeply, deeply proud.

I don't deny that today I can get picked up on some of this stuff by my super-smart daughter, Leyana. She ticks me off if she thinks I'm asking her to do something that I might equally ask of her brothers. She's right, of course, and I learn from her in the same way I've learnt from so many women. But if a woman today chooses the kind of traditional married life where she does everything for her husband and family, you're not going to find me criticising her. I'll support her every step of the way, if that's the life she wants to lead.

Coercion is where I draw the line: no one has the right to make someone else do something they don't want to do.

These nuances may be more complex in our Asian community than in white British communities, which is why we all need to be vigilant, to be aware of our own cultural preconceptions when we come to criticise or even legislate over others.

I will never forget the prejudices on display among the white judiciary at Mum's appeal.

The expectations placed on my mother, the role of service she was expected to provide, went too far. In the end, Mum became conditioned to believe that she had no choice but to accede to the brute force of violent men.

Lee remained in the house we'd bought together and, after a brief period of living with Foz, I moved into my own cottage. Leyana was seven, Aydan was just three and little Raese was still a baby. I had Mum to help, of course, which made a huge difference. My brother and my sister lived around the corner and my good friends were close by. I didn't need to stay in a marriage that wasn't working. I could survive on my own. I'd survived before.

And that's pretty much what I did. Seen from today's vantage point, the next four years swept by in a daze. I was so busy trying to keep all my plates spinning I didn't have a second to think about the future. Between 2010 and 2014, I kept the play centre going, always the first on site, always the last to leave. I had two kids in school and a toddler who needed my constant attention. But somehow I managed. As any small business owner will tell you, there's never enough time in the day to do all the things you have to do. I felt like a mouse on a treadmill.

Once more, resilience won the day. My mum had survived fourteen years in prison; my siblings had survived growing up without a mother and with their big sister cracking the whip. It didn't occur to me for a second during those four chaotic years that I wouldn't keep going. It's in my very nature to keep the wheels turning of whatever vehicle I'm driving. It didn't strike me as remotely strange that, just eighteen months earlier, I'd been a well-paid senior NHS commissioning professional and now I was washing sticky handprints off climbing frames. It didn't seem odd to me that I'd spent weeks on the Transformational Leadership Programme along with twenty-three other ambitious, successful professionals discussing the intricacies of leadership techniques, and now I was trying to persuade the landlord not to foreclose on the play centre because there wasn't enough cash in the business to pay the rent that month.

When you come from a working-class background – a working-class ethnic minority background, at that – you have absolutely no sense of entitlement. Every step of the journey of your life has to be fought for, because there ain't no plan B. I never for a moment thought: I'm a health sector professional, I have status, experience; I should be an executive and be well remunerated for my skills. I shouldn't be up late at night filling in my own tax return while simultaneously fixing the tears in my daughter's clothing.

I never for a minute forgot how lucky I was to be bringing a salary home at all. The working class often don't have the luxury of choice as to what job best suits their lifestyle.

When an MP stands up in Parliament and says there are plenty of jobs out there as long as you're prepared to take them, they don't take into account the day-to-day lives of many of the unemployed. There may be jobs available at Amazon warehouses, but if your 'local' warehouse is miles away from your house and there aren't enough buses to cover the route, then a huge part of your day would be spent travelling. If you're a parent and responsible for young children, how would you manage your childcare duties on top of all that travel? While there might be jobs to be had, that job must fit into the existing demands on your time, and those jobs are much harder to come by. Inaccessible work makes life harder, not easier, and pulling yourself together and taking what's out there is often not the best advice.

While ministers don't need to have suffered poverty to relate to their less well-off constituents, they do need to have empathy – a great lesson I learnt while working for the Samaritans. Working-class people don't hate wealth, they just don't have the same opportunities to make wealth; true equality is ensuring access to opportunity.

Poverty is a class issue and once its roots are embedded in you and your family, those roots will use all their strength to hold you down, to keep you in your place. This isn't politicking, it's simply the truth. And we either accept that truth and look no further, or we accept that truth and commit ourselves to working to change it.

I was struggling to cope, but I was putting one foot in front of the other, as I'd always done. I was running the play centre, raising my kids and making time for Mum. Very soon, I would be asking myself this question: was the tribunal the experience I needed in order to be ready for the politics train that was coming round the corner? Maybe. I certainly wasn't expecting it, imagining it or thinking about the possibility for even one second.

HONOURED

Nothing would have been further from my mind back in 2014.

And then I was invited to a meeting above a restaurant.

16

A Meeting Above a Restaurant

The 2012 by-election in Bradford West had been triggered by the ill-health of the Labour incumbent MP, Marsha Singh. Two years previously, Marsha had held the seat for Labour with a majority of almost six thousand votes. The far-left Respect Party, formed in 2004 by Salma Yaqoob and George Monbiot, was fielding a man called George Galloway as their candidate.

Surprise turned to shock when Marsha's majority was shattered, with Galloway beating the deputy leader of the Labour council, Imran Hussain, by over 10,000 votes. This was a seismic event in British politics, a cataclysmic failure for the Labour Party. Not for nothing did Galloway spend the next few months in interviews saying that he had initiated the 'Bradford Spring', a typically egotistical reference to the Arab Spring of two years earlier, implying a political uprising against the powerful Bradford political families known as the baradari.

You might say that Pakistani politics had been imported into Bradford. I've mentioned earlier how the big, powerful families in Pakistan became big, powerful families in Bradford, heavily involved in local politics and courted for their support from all corners of the community.

Take the Bradford Riots of July 2001. Tension between British Asian communities and far-right groups escalated, eventually erupting into violent confrontation. In the aftermath, political leaders – mostly white – began reaching out to our so-called community leaders: the baradari. In any other community, it's the people on the ground you'd seek feedback from – those whose voices of dissent are the most relevant. Voices that should, crucially, include women. But women are not part of the baradari demographic in any meaningful sense. So, instead of an honest and representative account of the causes behind the riots, what emerged was a selective interpretation – shaped by the 'respect' afforded to these powerful families.

This, right here, is how gatekeepers are created. Not in spite of culturally sensitive approaches, but because of them.

Cultural sensitivity is responsible for many of the ills in my community. Let's look at another example: female genital mutilation. If FGM was happening in mainstream society, it would clearly be understood as child abuse and outlawed immediately. While it's happening in marginal communities, it's viewed as a culturally sensitive issue and the powers that be tread very carefully. It's a racist framework: why should child abuse – like that seen in cultures where FGM is practised – be treated any differently from abuse in mainstream society?

Bradford is riddled with baradari politics and it's certainly been the bane of my life.

George Galloway saw an opportunity to rise against the influence of these families, calling it his 'Bradford Spring'. He wasn't alone in his ambition and the wider electorate too was growing tired of the baradari patriarchy running the city.

A MEETING ABOVE A RESTAURANT

Nepotism exists everywhere – particularly in government, where connections often drive political ideology. Where it's different with baradari politics is that it's driven by families and family power. And once again izzat comes into play: the honour of the family and their pride.

Galloway's ambition won him the seat. I even voted for him.

In 2012, I was trying to make ends meet with the Monster Fun play centre and being a single parent to three kids. I was way too busy to think about politics, to even poke my head up above the towering parapet. And when I did briefly surface for air, it was to watch George Galloway rock into town on his campaign bus. His criticism of the baradari system of clan politics was, to me, the key thrust of his campaign.

In 2014, during the time of the Gaza War, I found myself getting heavily involved in support for Palestine. I arranged a convoy to go from Bradford to protest outside the BBC in Manchester, drawing on the campaigning techniques I'd developed all those years ago when working with Southall Black Sisters and Justice for Women. But that was the extent of my politics in 2014 – I didn't meet George Galloway at all during the period he was an MP for Bradford West. I didn't have much of a political instinct in those days and I knew nothing about Westminster. I knew nothing about the interminable squabbles between politicians on TV.

I had no background in political history, so I didn't know that the Respect Party had arisen out of factionalised fighting on the left after the Tony Blair years of moderation. The one thing I did know was that the patriarchal clans stifle all opportunities for women in Bradford, so anyone who opposed it got my wholehearted approval – and the approval of many other women. At a fundamental level, we knew enough about how it worked in Bradford to understand that the male politicians were damaging the city. They were mainly representing their own business interests.

What perhaps many of us didn't appreciate back in 2012 was that George Galloway's performance – his way of sweeping into town like our saviour, running around in his battle bus for sixteen days of campaigning – was very much his modus operandi. Brilliant with the photo opportunities and the soundbites, but in my opinion not so great on the day-to-day responsibilities of being a constituency MP. His voting record in Parliament was just 11 per cent. To give a sense of how unacceptable this percentage is, I was once pulled up when my voting record fell below 90 per cent, even though it was due to genuine ill health and periods of hospitalisation.

It's true that he tabled a huge number of Early Day Motions, questions raised in Parliament to highlight the concerns of constituents, but in themselves, they don't amount to very much. They are statements of intent, and I think Galloway would use these Early Day Motions to demonstrate his representation of West Bradford, but it was busywork. It was all talk and no action. And to top it all, we hardly ever saw him.

On 1 June 2014, the Labour MP for Birmingham Perry Bar, Khalid Mahmood, came to Bradford to try to find a solution to 'the Galloway issue'. It had been posited that at the heart of Labour's failure to address some of the fundamental economic injustices of the city lay the entire issue of baradari.

A MEETING ABOVE A RESTAURANT

Essentially, one family were controlling the key council positions in Bradford West and distributing those positions to the men within or under the control of that family.

Labour decided that the best way to deal with this problem was to turn Bradford West into an all-women shortlist and Khalid Mahmood was given the job of finding the women who might be prepared to take on George Galloway at the next election to be become the MP for Bradford West.

I had been approached by a friend of mine, Sabiya Khan, to attend that meeting of women.

Summoned to Mumtaz, a local Indian restaurant, I arrived at the same time as four other women. Straight away we were ushered upstairs, while the Birmingham Perry Bar MP, Khalid Mahmood (although I didn't even know who he was at that point), sat downstairs with other men from the community.

Why an all-woman shortlist? The Labour Party had two problems: one was George Galloway, the other was baradari politics. They knew they had lost the seat due to those politics, and that a woman would be an ideal candidate to keep out the baradari, as the baradari had never put forward a woman to stand in an election. It was a way to kill two birds with one stone. We women were the stones.

Back in the restaurant, no one offered us a drink or a bite to eat. 'Just wait', we were told. 'Khalid will be with you very shortly.'

By now, I was really cheesed off. It was a Sunday night, I had to get my kids to bed, what was I even doing here? So much for involving women in Bradford politics.

Eventually, Khalid made his way upstairs. He was full of smiles and good cheer.

But I have never been one to hold my tongue. 'Why on earth did you think it was OK to stick us in this room, waiting for you to grace us with your company?' I asked him.

That got his back up immediately. He didn't answer me, but instead asked, 'Which one of you is going to take on George Galloway?' So that's why we were here.

The four other women declined on the spot. Galloway, it has to be said, was perceived as a tough campaigner. Who'd want to get into a fight with him?

I looked at Khalid and said, 'I could chew him up and spit him out.'

He returned a look that clearly said, *Who the hell do you think you are?*

I held his eye, in all my cocky splendour.

'Oh, you could, could you?'

'Easy.'

'So tell me what's wrong with Bradford?' he asked in his strong Brummie accent.

'Racism, of course!' I exclaimed. 'That's what's wrong with Bradford.'

'What?' He was riled.

'Give me a second and I'll tell you,' I said, getting into my groove. 'You have councillors who don't speak fluent English yet still occupy positions of power. They should be holding people to account and scrutinising the budgets and reports that affect the lives of thousands of people across this city, but they're more interested in hanging on to their status than running their departments. Why is no one challenging baradari clan politics? Because it's culturally sensitive? Well, that is just plain racist. When these councillors don't challenge issues like forced marriage and honour crimes because it's a cultural issue, that's racism!'

He was trying to get a word in, but I was on a roll.

'You've got people in power who keep others in power not because of meritocracy or ability but because they give you, the Labour MP of their choosing, the baradari block vote,' I continued. 'We're almost at the bottom of the barrel when it comes to education, with no sign of any accountability, and then you ask what's wrong with Bradford. That's what's wrong with Bradford!'

My rant was over.

'Why aren't you in politics?' Khalid asked.

'Because it's a man's world and it's the dirtiest place to be,' I snapped, my frustration getting the better of me.

To which again, he responded very calmly: 'Well, if you're not going to get involved, then who's going to clean it up?'

The next day, I sent Khalid my CV. He offered to put me through a Labour Party leadership course and told me I could be ready to stand for Parliament in five years' time. I thought he was joking. 'You want me to apply for a job that pays me less than I would earn if I went back into my old job, and you want me to wait five years before I can even apply?'

That was not going to happen. I went on, 'I probably already know more about leadership than you do. Put me up for the election next year and I'll consider standing; otherwise I'm not interested.'

I had the experience: I'd been a senior manager in the NHS and a regional director in a local government association; I knew the city and had all the right leadership skills. I knew I could do it, and I knew I could do a better job for the people of Bradford West than George Galloway.

Soon, I was on my way to London and found myself at a celebratory Eid dinner in a big hotel in Park Lane, attended by the likes of Ed Miliband. It was here I witnessed a Muslim woman, Shabana Mahmood, MP for Birmingham Ladywood, introducing the event. It was an inspiration and a game-changer for me. Here was a woman of faith holding her own before the great and the good. This was the first dip of my toe into the big pond. So this is what power looks like, I thought, gazing round the room at all those men and women in politics.

My other thought: I want a piece of this. I liked this world.

And it was good timing – I had the head space to consider a change of direction now that Mum was free. But I had no clue exactly how it would impact my life.

My family's opinion about this new direction? By now they were resigned to fact that I'm gonna do what I'm gonna do.

The rest, as they say, is history.

On 2 March 2015, I was selected to be the parliamentary candidate for Bradford West. Politics is a rough old game and soon I was to discover just how rough it could really be.

17

Dreams of My Mother

I had eight weeks to get ready.

Maybe that doesn't sound too bad – two months should have been ample time to prepare the ground for my candidacy – but I'd never been involved in politics before. I had no idea what I was supposed to be doing. I'd been selected as the Labour candidate for Bradford West on 2 March, the general election was going to be held on 7 May and in between I had to become the name on everyone's lips if I was going to stand a chance of winning.

For the first few days, at home in Bradford, I made many phone calls, asking for lots of advice from the party about my next steps. But I spent most of my time wondering how I could optimise my chance of getting elected and how I should go about it. Of course, I had all my campaigning experience – I knew how to talk to people and get my point across succinctly and persuasively. But I was going head-to-head with a seasoned campaigner in Galloway. I'd need to be better, smarter and quicker than him from the off.

I hadn't given the practical side of becoming an MP much thought – that was a problem for the future, should I be successful. But I assumed that Lee would step into any breach as and when he was needed during the three days a week I'd have to spend in London.

Of course, I'd completely underestimated what the job would entail in terms of the demands on my time – votes in the House going on late into the night, my days subject to change at any point because of questions in the chamber. I had watched a few TV programmes that unpacked for a lay audience how Parliament works, but that was pretty much the extent of my rudimentary research. There was no way I could appreciate the sheer commitment required, given I had three kids – at the time they were three, eight and twelve years old.

There was some surprise in Bradford at my selection and, from the usual baradari family quarters, a distinctly unenthusiastic reaction. Who was this Naz Shah with her big claims about how she's going to beat George Galloway?

After a few days of pondering the direction my campaign would take, I decided that the best thing I could do was to introduce myself to the people of Bradford West and, in particular, the women of Bradford West. I knew very well that I wasn't the only female who disliked the patriarchal attitudes of the Bradford men back then, and I'm certainly not the only one now.

On Sunday, 8 March 2015, International Women's Day, I wrote a blog entitled 'Dreams of My Mother and Dreams for My Daughter' – the title, of course, inspired by Barack Obama's memoir, *Dreams from My Father*. Published in association with one of the local newspapers, within days it went viral.

Much of the content of the blog you will already be familiar with having read thus far, but I think it's worth including

DREAMS OF MY MOTHER

this small extract to show how I was feeling about going into politics:

> Last week, I was selected to stand as the prospective parliamentary candidate for Bradford West, where I was born and raised, and where I live and am raising my own family.
>
> In my first press interview the reporter asked me what brought me into politics and referred to my own life story. Later on that evening, on the journey back from London, my friend asked me how I felt. I responded I would know once I was in my mother's arms. I also explained that I had many years ago read Barack Obama's *Dreams from My Father*, and for me to be where I am today were the dreams of my mother.
>
> I was only six when my father abandoned my mother with two young children and pregnant with a third, eloping with the neighbour's sixteen-year-old daughter. When my father left my mother, it was my mother who was ostracised and persecuted. Every chapter of her life following her marriage is a book in itself, how her husband refused to pick up her first child because she was a girl, how she was battered by her husband, how she lost children due to beatings.
>
> How she lost all her izzat when she was on the front page of the local rag as a murderer and sentenced to twenty years. She laid bare for the whole world to see her wounds from sexual exploitation at an appeal only to be dismissed as incapable of belief and then once again before the Lord Chief Justice, who finally accepted she was driven to kill, and he reduced her tariff.

My selection isn't about me; it's about the recognition of inequality in society. It's an understanding that we still have many changes to make. It's my way of making things right because if I've learnt anything I have learnt that through compassion we can change the world. We cannot change things through just complaining; we must be part of the solution and we must have conversations, real meaningful and honest conversations not only with ourselves but with our families, our communities and beyond.

I've always campaigned against violence against women and have a deep understanding of the role of 'power and control', but even I have been taken aback by the 'power dynamics' of politics. I had not reached home following my selection and I had at least two new fake Twitter accounts set up in my name. Already my 'character' has been attacked and desecrated through social media and trolling. The smear campaign that has started has been some of the most vicious and disgusting I have seen. But it does not scare me, will not change me, and it in fact fuels my passion for change more.

Even in a short space of just six days this tells me clearly that unfortunately twenty-two years later it is still a woman's character that is attacked. Why is it that men's characters are not questioned in this city when they stand for elections? For me personally, every attack is a further indictment of why I must stand and challenge the status quo, it gives me more strength and resilience to ensure I win the trust and belief of the people in Bradford West and then this election to bring change in my community.

Today is also International Women's Day and I will be

speaking at a conference as well as my first hustings. Each bit of my story and the celebration of women across the world overwhelms me that little bit more today.

When I did finally get home the night I was selected, my mother sat up in her bed and held me close while I cried. We cried together knowing that while my past and my present are the dreams of my mother and her inspiration for me, my future is about the dreams I have for my own daughter, she is my inspiration to bring change and equality for the world in which she is growing up, the community we live in and the wider society.

After that blog went live, everything changed.

Once my blog went viral, everyone wanted to talk to me. I was on Channel Four News, the BBC, and the press wanted interviews. Galloway, I suspect, had reassured himself that given Labour had selected a nobody to stand against him, he was going to win as easily as he had before in 2012. But suddenly, he had a serious opponent.

Bradford West became a hugely significant vote. Overnight, it went from being just one of 650 contested seats in a general election to the status of a by-election. When he defeated Imran Hussain in 2012, Galloway, having already boasted that his victory was akin to the Arab Spring, was intimating that he had single-handedly changed the political landscape. Now, everyone was asking if this newcomer – this unknown working-class Bradford woman with a colourful backstory – could restore the pride of the Labour movement to Bradford. By 2015, Galloway proved that none of his ambition to reform the baradari had any merit. This time around, he went straight to the community leaders to ask for their support against me.

While I had never doubted it for a second, I remained determined to sustain the energy my blog had inspired. I never wavered in my belief that I could beat the incumbent MP: not for one second after that cocky conversation I'd had above the Mumtaz restaurant with Khalid Mahmood did I ever think I would lose against Galloway. This wasn't about arrogance.

I engaged in *istikhara*, a prayer asking God for guidance, whereby God will show you the way forward. Either your path will be strewn with problems, which is God's way of telling you that you've made the wrong choice, or you will find things falling into place as you move through your life. Once I had completed my istikhara, things began to go my way, indicating that this was the right path for me. I therefore believed that God wished me to stand against Galloway and that He might favour my case as long as I retained my authenticity and my humility. In Islam, we believe that if you act with honesty and integrity while keeping your focus on doing good, then your efforts will find favour. And whatever anyone's views on George Galloway, the people of Bradford West had had three years to discover that he wasn't very interested in representing the needs of his constituents, as he was never there for them.

That, in effect, became the theme of my campaign. At the very first hustings (a meeting for candidates to talk directly to the voters) in a noisy, boisterous room – Galloway always makes a lot of noise as a campaigner and his supporters always make a lot of noise too; it's one of the techniques he uses to intimidate others – I took the mic. I looked across the crowded hall, and said: 'Oh, look over there – it's our absentee MP! We don't usually see very much of him much in Bradford.'

That was all I needed to say. The whole room took a sharp intake of breath. From that moment, Galloway was on the back foot. All you had to do was look at his voting record in Parliament, look at how many debates in the Commons he actually attended and participated in, and then look at how many outside media interests he had. You didn't need to be a political genius to see that George Galloway was all about George Galloway.

Then he made his next mistake. After I sat down, he got to his feet. He waved a piece of paper in my direction. He announced to the room that he was holding the nikah or marriage certificate for my marriage to Mazhar.

'She's a liar!' he told the hall.

The certificate he was holding was for the second nikah, performed when I had returned to Pakistan at the age of sixteen. He was claiming that I hadn't been forced into marriage at the age of fifteen; that I'd married at sixteen and my mum was present and therefore knew what I was doing. He was trying to suggest that my entire backstory was made up. That I'd manipulated facts about my life to make me a more authentic character, a more relatable candidate to the local population.

There was uproar in the hall, but he'd made a fatal, stupid error which would be simple to correct. Pragna Patel of Southall Black Sisters and Shaista Gohir of Muslim Women's Network UK both put out statements in my defence. Even the Tory peer Baroness Warsi came out against George Galloway's attack. I, however, didn't respond. I simply let Galloway bury himself. And that's what he did. He buried himself, without me needing to say a word.

Yes, my mum had been present when I married Mazhar, but that in itself meant nothing. Had he never heard of parents forcing their kids into marriage? Not that Mum had forced me; I had been ordered to marry Mazhar to heal a family rift, which was coercion enough.

With that foolish and bullying tactic, Galloway had undone much of the good work that the cross-faith community had focused on the wider issue of forced marriages. He'd shown himself for what he was: a self-interested attack dog and, in the eyes of many women, a misogynist. That very big mistake he made at the hustings brought me a wave of support from women's groups, who were appalled at the way he had seemingly rolled back all the years of effort they had ploughed into supporting women faced with little choice but to marry the partner selected by their elders.

From that very first hustings, I stayed visible. Wherever I went in the constituency, the next day Galloway would rock up in his tour bus. He was never the first on the ground, always second.

He was also losing on the issue of baradari. I, too, was vocal in my criticism of the clan politics but mine was a genuine local voice. I was raised here; Bradford was my home. Bradford women in particular seemed to respond to me, and you could feel Galloway's authenticity draining away.

I also got some crucial support from Labour Party big hitters such as Lord Roy Kennedy and Baroness Glenys Thornton, who organised and led the campaigning. It was a very different methodology to the patriarchal approach of the baradari men of the Labour Party in Bradford. I learnt how to apply modern data-gathering techniques. We weren't just knocking on random doors and chatting, we were scientific in our approach, noting who was for me, who was against and who was undecided. Together, we set up meetings, photo-ops, hustings and organised volunteers. I added to this my own particular campaigning tool: I asked every woman I spoke to, who had pledged to vote for me, to take my message to at least two of her friends in the hope they would be convinced by my message and vote for me too. And, if so, they should speak to two of their friends in turn.

We'd set the pace of the campaign with the viral blog, but we had been in front from the very start by highlighting Galloway's record. I was given some crucial support from members of the Labour Women's Network such as Rachel Reeves and Yvette Cooper. Even Sadiq Khan came to open my first election campaign office. We needed a professional profile to minimise the impact of the local baradari families and their short-sighted, misogynistic attacks on me. But more than anything, I relied on getting out into the community and talking to constituents.

It was a tough campaign; Galloway was, and I'm sure still is, an aggressive campaigner and every time we met to face each other at the hustings, I needed to be strong. Every day, I'd wake up in the morning and feel sick. I wasn't scared of the challenge – I still believed I would win – but it was rough, it was nasty and it was all very, very high profile. I had so many leading Labour lights arriving in the city to walk around Bradford with me, I hadn't quite taken on board how important it was for the Party to demonstrate the fallibility of the Respect proposition. We had to show that Galloway wasn't offering the community anything of value, that he was an absentee MP with an appalling voting record, and that he didn't represent the people of Bradford West in Parliament to the best of his ability. Part of my strategy was to unpick his empty promises to his constituents.

It was a dirty fight.

My campaign team did their best to protect me from the worst attacks on my character until after the election. We were all in agreement that nothing should derail my focus. However, now and then I would come face to face with underhand tactics aimed at destabilising the campaign.

One morning, opening the back door of my house to enter the garden, I almost trod on a dead crow, its mouth stuffed with grass. A nasty, feral warning with a strong whiff of a dark omen about it. To access the back of my house, someone must have climbed up and over the high garden fence. Boy, they really wanted to scare me. I also found out this wasn't the first time a dead crow had been sent to scare me – in the past, members of my team had disposed of the malicious evidence before I could see it.

The vitriol kept coming. Even my dad's widow hosted an event for Galloway. By involving herself in the election campaign, she had exposed me to speculation of the worst kind. I was Naz Shah, prospective Labour candidate for Bradford West, whose father had run off with a sixteen-year-old. She actually told a local journalist that she had been just fifteen when she first fell in love with my father. I had never mentioned the age of the girl my father ran off with, and now it was all anyone could talk about.

My father's family promptly ostracised me – the press were

calling my dad a groomer. And somehow I was responsible! I hadn't abandoned my family. I hadn't left my children destitute while I ran off with a girl less than half my age. But I shouldn't have been surprised; this was the way it had always been. Men commit the shame and women take the blame.

Despite the gossip, the rumours and the downright lies, I had many Labour professionals on side. And because we always led from the front – never on the back foot, never reactionary – we made steady progress.

It was often painful, and I was taken aback by the spite of some of the attacks upon me and my family. My mother's history, of course, was rehashed in lurid ways on different social media platforms and I was thankful that she had no access to those forums. Lee was offered money to 'kiss and tell', while Mum endured silent phone calls in the middle of the night. It would be understandable to assume that my mum might have been appalled by the publicity, by the fact that her past had been raked up and misrepresented. It would be understandable to assume she just wanted a quiet life now, out of the public gaze, left alone to help raise her grandchildren. The truth was quite the opposite. Mum never once asked me to stop campaigning. If anything, she encouraged me to fight harder. She saw my victory as way to reclaim her own izzat, to stand tall and proud of her daughter's achievements.

Mum never quite got the public recognition that she was a victim. It was an injustice she couldn't bear, and now that I was on the receiving end of the nasty tactics of our opponents, she was furious. It would be fair to say that much of my passion, my desire for justice and equality, hails directly from my mother.

An anonymous blog appeared online, painting both Mum and me as sexual deviants. This was the last straw for Foz. 'I can't wait for this all to be over!' she raged.

It was Foz who struggled hardest with my campaign and as a result she wasn't always supportive. She was too busy dealing with the impact of the dirty tricks of those who wanted to see me fail. When my blog went viral, the backlash had been too much for her. She wanted the sort of life you'd think Mum was craving – out of the public eye, invisible at last.

Foz watched all the bridges crumble that we'd built over the years and since Mum's release, as our extended family and certain community members shunned us once more for bringing unwanted attention to the Shah name.

'What will you do if she wins?' Foz's best friend asked her.

'If she wins?' Foz asked, puzzled.

'Well,' piped up Imy, 'she might. I even had a dream where we were all celebrating,'

It hadn't occurred to Foz that I might be successful. It hadn't even crossed her mind. She hated the dogged smears against my character – that I was a non-respectful, party-loving girl, because every now and then I liked a dance. But that was weak stuff compared to some of the foul comments on the anonymous blog. Foz wasn't entirely alone in her despair; most mornings I'd be putting on my best face in the bathroom after being sick in the sink.

But I faced down the intimidation, swept away the dead crows on my doorstep and ignored the vile slanders against my mum. And it was bolstering to feel so much love and support in my community too. One day on the campaign trail, I knocked on a door and was faced with a beaming husband and wife. 'Kids, come and see Naz,' the mum called into the back room. 'We're all voting for you, don't worry,' she told me. Well, I just burst into tears. To be shown kindness amid all the vitriol was too much.

The baradari families may have feared my possible election, but even within those powerful networks there were men who publicly supported me. Men who wanted real change in West Bradford and who believed I could deliver it. You can't win an election with just women on your side – to win, you need the men's votes too. I have never shied away from criticising the bad seeds in our community for fear of reinforcing Islamophobic tropes or defending the indefensible. Quite the contrary. It's my job to chase the truth, to correct lies. For every arsehole who tries to push his patriarchal agenda on me and other women, there are many, many more men who stand firm in support.

Bradford has suffered from being judged by the actions of a few, as though a handful of villains represent the whole city. This election had to be a win not only for me but for the good men too. The support I received from businesses across Bradford was phenomenal.

But it was the support from members of a prominent baradari family that really took my breath away. Rizwan Malik and Shabs Hussein – baradari men through and through – put their faith in me and effectively broke rank with their peers.

Enraged by the Labour Party for the omission of their preferred candidate, the baradari men had met and many had decided to switch their allegiance to an outside candidate from London. Riz and Shabs insisted they support someone local, that it wasn't my fault their candidate hadn't been selected, and I shouldn't be held responsible.

Riz gave me his word that he would stand by me against the baradari system, should I be selected. I was and he did. He wanted to break the strong arm of clan politics and for the gatekeepers to lose their power. And he commanded enough respect in the community to convince others to give me a chance.

Both Riz and Shabs have supported me ever since. To this day, Riz still drives me around the polling stations in Bradford West on election day.

In the end, it was resilience and leadership that prevailed. The same strategies that had helped me overcome challenges in my personal life and drive my career forward were with me every single day of the 2015 campaign.

Which leads us back to the beginning of this book and that very special evening when Foz, Imy and I gathered at his house to pray the night before the election. A night I will never forget.

I wrote two speeches – one for victory and one for defeat – just as I had been advised. In truth, I never doubted I would win. Every day of that campaign, out on the streets of my home city, I could feel the momentum building: change was in the air. On election night, I put on my best dress and turned up at the Richard Dunn Sports Centre to hear the results. I stood there motionless as the announcement came: we had overturned Galloway's 10,000-vote majority and secured a Labour victory with a majority of 11,420. The hall erupted. A thrill of victory surged through me like an electric shock.

As I stood there, Galloway took to the podium and

delivered a strange runner-up speech — if I remember correctly, it involved something about hyenas and lions. *You had it coming*, I thought. The people of Bradford West have seen through you. And they've just done me the greatest honour of my life.

I was now the Member of Parliament for my hometown.

When it was all over, I went back to my brother's house and was met by a staggering number of four-by-fours parked outside. Everyone was there — my supporters *and* my detractors. Even those who had been judgemental about Mum's imprisonment and my campaigning arrived with congratulations and gifts. An old saying sprang to mind: success has many fathers, where failure remains an orphan. Never a truer phrase was uttered.

Mum was beside herself for most of the evening, saying, 'These people had vilified me, and now they turn up with sweets.'

She wasn't bitter, though. She's not a bitter woman — how would she have survived if she was? She was proud of me and the respect my election commanded.

Mum had never once stopped praying. Every single day of those fourteen years in prison, she performed namaz. She turned to God for comfort, for reassurance, and now He was rewarding her with success. She could hold her head up in the community and she was magnanimous, never once turning away those who had once slandered her. Quite the opposite — she lavished them with kindness. Because that's who she is.

Mum is the living embodiment of the Muslim concept of *tawakkul*, the surrender of yourself to God's will, while accepting that it is God who makes the best plans for His creation, not humans. That whatever good or bad thing befalls you has been sent from God and is His will. We live our lives with good intentions and kindness towards others. If you have good wishes in your heart, then only goodness will come back to you. The level of forgiveness my family exerts is monumental.

Technically, we should be very bitter. We should be resentful of the treatment we received, both in the courts of law and from our extended family and the community who rejected us. And yet we still crave acceptance and validation from that very same community. My religion is about family and community; that is where we make our strongest emotional commitments.

It's true that Foz had a very hard time being back in the public eye. She was particularly angry with my stepmother, who had campaigned against me. But by the time election day rolled round, her anger had evaporated and she accepted that whatever happened came from God and she didn't have the wisdom to challenge His wishes. It was also about acknowledging that while I bared my soul and my pain in a viral blog, my father had three other children and their memories of him were of an entirely different order.

If we accept this premise that we may plan but God's plans are always better, there isn't much room for bitterness. It's like a magic pill that allows you to centre yourself in your faith. This is what we preach. God has blessed me not only with good things but also no small share of adversity. The result is that my resilience knows no bounds.

While Mum acknowledges her pain and the incredible injustice she suffered, her view is: *Look what God has gifted me in return.* But we don't own our success, we accept that God could take it away. When tawakkul is part of your life in this way, you don't have an attachment to status, to ego, to money. But we're only human and we can't help but be pissed off if bad things happen – tawakkul is about finding contentment that is rooted in faith, not in material or physical pleasures, not in wealth. No matter how bad things are, we return to the premise that it's all OK. It's all part of God's plan.

It cuts deep when someone hurts me, don't get me wrong. And I have felt suicidal in the past. But each time I come back to the trials and tribulations of our Prophet, Muhammad, peace be upon him, and they give me the strength not only to continue, but to use that despair to drive me forward. You can accept your despair, but you have to hold on to your tawakkul. It's the beauty of life, the beauty of tragedy, that gives you the tools to emerge stronger than ever.

How would we ever appreciate the gift of our resilience if we hadn't had to battle now and then?

Resilience is a strength – an armour that allows you to return to battle when others might see only defeat. It's a resource I call on virtually every day. As a brown-skinned, working-class woman who left school at the age of twelve, I encounter both conscious and unconscious bias constantly. But when you've spent a lifetime facing discrimination and rejection, you learn to build a deep well of resilience to draw from when you need it most.

I want my kids to be resilient. I want our leaders to show resilience in the face of the increasingly toxic tone of public debate. And I wish the gift of resilience to everyone who faces challenges in their lives.

Seeing the election party in full swing and Mum beaming broadly all evening was exactly the encouragement I needed to embrace my new role wholeheartedly. She had ignited something in my spirit long ago, a small flame that grew brighter as I fought harder for her. I would do her proud, I promised myself.

So there I was, a mandated Member of Parliament. God had sent me a great gift, I had a purpose and I was going to do everything in my power to deliver success to my community – whether they had voted for me or not.

18

Member of Parliament

And so a new career path beckoned – one that took me to the hallowed halls of Westminster.

Growing up in poverty in a working-class family can define a mindset that never truly leaves you. I'm not talking about the proverbial 'chip on the shoulder'; I'm always genuinely pleased when people flourish at what they want to excel in and I don't care whether they grew up in a backstreet two-up, two-down or a palace.

But mine is the sort of background that sticks to you. You're never able to forget your origins, because society – and this is very much a British phenomenon rather than an American one – cannot help but remind you of your roots. The smooth, rounded edges of middle-class professionals who have been to university, enjoyed gap years and holidayed in Italy will always feel unassailable to you. You will be picked up on for your poor vocabulary. Your experience of travel, of reading, of social events, will always be so limited compared to theirs. You will carry your roots with you everywhere you go.

But it's more than that. The British system is structured to maintain poverty among working-class communities.

This isn't about how I might feel while I'm sitting on the terrace of the House of Commons and someone makes a comment that I know is, in a very real way, a slight on my background. It's not about me. It's about how generations of working-class people in this country are held back by ingrained class structures that abandon them to poor housing and limited access to education, health care and job opportunities. As I said, it's no good politicians standing up in Westminster or on *Question Time* and insisting there are plenty of jobs around if you're just prepared to take them. Poverty is a class issue and once its roots are embedded in you and your family, those roots will use their musculature to hold you down, to keep you in your place. This isn't politicking, it's simply the truth. We can either ignore that truth or we acknowledge it and commit ourselves to working hard to change it and have more working-class MPs with real lived experiences; Dawn Butler and Angela Rayner come to mind.

When you're very poor, you put one foot in front of the other and you do what you need to do to get by. Millions and millions of us follow this path. That was certainly my life in those blurred, exhausting years in Bradford when I was trying to keep all those plates spinning. This juggling of plates was very much on my mind when I was elected to government. But politics? Nothing could have been further from my thoughts back in 2014 when I was invited to that meeting above a restaurant.

Nothing can quite prepare you for becoming a Member of Parliament in Britain. There are, of course, those gilded young men and women who have drifted into politics after successful stints in the debating society at their public school and the Oxford Union. They're easy to spot in Westminster – they look like they've just wandered in from their parents' sitting room, so comfortable are they in this environment. I was soon to learn that I had to think carefully about my clothes after various comments were made about my turning up in the same outfits, week after week.

For working-class MPs – and there are a good many of us from all political persuasions – it's impossible not to be awestruck by the faded opulence of the nineteenth-century Charles Barry Gothic Revival architecture. Other political arenas I have visited over the years, from Washington to Islamabad, feature more contemporary working environments. There is nothing about Westminster that suggests 'office' – it looks more like a set from an episode of *Downton Abbey*. Friendly doorkeepers wearing antiquated uniforms that feature golden accoutrements will show you the way if you're lost. There are shabby but elegant bars – so many bars! – replete with worn leather-trim seating, where florid-faced men and women knock back gin and tonics. Even the toilets were designed and installed over a century ago.

This grandeur, albeit a little worse for wear, was a million miles away from the working environments of my life up until that point – the restaurant, the launderette, the Seabrook crisps factory and the modern NHS offices where I worked for five years. I felt a powerful sense of displacement. It was genuinely bizarre to find myself sitting pretty in a building that might have inspired Hogwarts itself. There were so many times I had to pinch myself to remind me that this was real, that I had been selected by the people to be here.

At the same time, I wasn't in any way overawed or cowed by my surroundings. From the day of my election in May

2015, I have never – not for a single moment – felt imposter syndrome or experienced any sense of self-doubt. If anything, my sense of self-worth increased when I began to meet my fellow MPs and discovered that many of them had a shockingly limited experience of life and work. Maybe if I'd had the same opportunities, I'd be much further up the ladder. Where would they be now, had they walked in my shoes? Hadn't I earnt my place as the representative of the people of Bradford West, where I'd spent some forty years either struggling to survive or fighting to support others who had been cast aside by the world? I had absolutely no sense of being out of my depth. I had been appointed to look after the interests of the people I had grown up with, and I had been given that appointment because those people trusted me. Now it was my job to repay their trust.

After my election, the city of Bradford was already looking very different to me and my family. The Shahs, who for years had literally been pariahs, were now significant members of the Bradford community. In one stroke, I had effectively restored my mum's izzat.

We were invited to attend dinners, weddings and festive events to celebrate new babies. Someone once remarked to me, 'People aren't shaking your hand, Naz. They're shaking the hand of your *status*.' I won't deny it, it was satisfying to watch Mum enjoying *her* new status, too, and it was also satisfying for me to know that Imy and Foz were now granted additional status because they were the siblings of the local Member of Parliament. We had held open the door to our community, we had hung on to our roots and our home city throughout the bad times, and now the very community that had rejected us was opening its arms to us. That was how it felt; that's how it still feels.

I discovered that the emerging politician in me could sit companionably alongside the campaigner. I wouldn't soften my stance on the issues I believed in, and I never wanted to feel 'comfortable' as an MP. I have no desire for a 'comfortable' life if that means turning a blind eye to wrongdoing. As far as I'm concerned, justice and fairness override everything – even party politics. If something is wrong, then I'm happy to say it's wrong and do my best to put it right.

Let me give you an example, one that to this day I will think of at some point between waking up in the morning and closing my eyes at night.

In July 2016, during my second year as an MP, I was contacted by a constituent who recounted the story of a young Bradford woman – a British Pakistani named Samia Shahid who had been found dead in Punjab. Within a matter of minutes, it was clear to me that this was another so-called 'honour killing'. (What an epic misnomer that is – that murder is in any sense justified for *dishonouring* one's family.) This young woman was twenty-eight years old at the time of her death and had been through an arranged marriage which ultimately failed. She had separated from her husband, fallen in love with another man and remarried. While she had found happiness, her family had not. They were disgruntled to the point that one member commented that Samia may think she's safe in England, but if she ever goes back to Pakistan, she's a dead woman.

Samia had been living with her new husband in Dubai but had wanted to return to Pakistan to visit her father, who was in poor health. Her husband pleaded with her not to go, saying she wouldn't be safe. But Samia was a loyal daughter and wanted to try to make amends with her father before it was too late, even though he had been vocal in his disapproval of her divorce and remarriage. So she flew to Pakistan.

Two days later, Samia was dead.

Her father took a photograph of her body lying at the foot of the stairs; it was a tragic accident, he claimed. Conflicting stories emerged from the family: she had asthma, she'd had a heart attack, she'd tripped down the stairs.

I contacted Helen Pidd, a trusted and respected *Guardian* journalist, and briefed her on the case. Helen came up to Bradford and began asking questions of Samia's family, only to be met with a wall of silence and denial. Meanwhile, I got on to the embassy in Pakistan, and I made a direct call to their prime minister's office. I briefed some key campaigners – including the filmmaker Shameen Obaid-Chinoy, who had made a film on 'honour killing' – as well as some women's rights campaigners.

Once Helen had gone live with her story in the *Guardian*, I geared up for action. The Pakistani prime minister ordered an investigation into the police actions at the time of Samia's death, and a trail of police corruption was uncovered. Crucial evidence had been withheld. Within days, Samia's father and her first husband confessed to her murder – she had been asphyxiated with a plastic bag after being raped by her ex-husband.

It was at this point the detective warned me that his force had received a threat against my life. When I asked why there had been a death threat made against me, I was told: 'Because you've been poking your nose into places you shouldn't.'

Was he actually telling me off?

'Let's start again, officer,' I said. 'I'll poke my nose where I want, I'm an elected Member of Parliament. Isn't it your job to protect me?'

To his credit, he realised that he'd made an error, that his flippancy was exactly the sort of comment that keeps justice at bay.

'If I can't poke my nose into the murder of an innocent young woman,' I carried on, 'then I should be ashamed of myself and you should be ashamed of yourself for suggesting otherwise.'

For me, as for so many women in Bradford, and for many other campaigners and social justice advocates in the UK and around the world, leadership means stepping in when there is a clear-cut case for intervention. Whether Samia had been young or old, brown, Black or white, her beautiful life had been cut short and she deserved justice. Without justice, we have no way of assuring our children that the world is a safe place in which to grow up. It is our responsibility to ensure our kids understand that cycles of bad behaviour – in whatever culture, class or creed they originate – cannot be sanctioned. And the actions of Pakistan's prime minister, and those of the police, demonstrated that a positive outcome could come out of a horrific tragedy.

The fight goes on. Every July, I raise the anniversary of Samia's killing, because we must never allow the memory of what happened to her to be erased.

You may not be surprised to hear that there are still people in Bradford who believe I shouldn't continue to remind the world of her murder, that it's time to shut up.

Well, I won't.

What I learnt from this episode was that having the platform of an elected MP gave me power, magnified my voice and allowed the words I spoke to be heard. I had earnt a rare space through my election; having the mandate of the people is enormously effective. In a democracy, the engine driving your agenda comes from the people who made you an MP. And when you have their support in the polling booths, you are gifted the level of confidence you need to do your job to the best of your ability and to hold others to account. And it was this confidence, this mandate, that gave me the platform to profile Samia's case so successfully.

There are an estimated 2 billion Muslims in the world today – about a quarter of the global population. Wherever we live, we stand for core values: patriotism, fairness, justice and equality. In the UK, British Muslims serve in Parliament, represent our nation in sport, care for patients as doctors and nurses, teach in our schools and help shape the future as leaders. We are British and proud of it, and we are also people of faith – just like any other religious community in this country. By taking a broader leadership role in global Muslim affairs, I hope that I have served not only my own community in Bradford but also given my constituents something to be proud of – and something to hold on to – when the tempers of division flare.

I also hope I have shown the constituents of Bradford West who aren't Muslims that my commitment is equally to them. Discrimination on the basis of religion or race is unacceptable –

wherever and however it occurs. My dream is that we come together as one single community, united by shared values regardless of faith or belief.

There will always be more to do. At some point, every person – of any culture, faith or none at all – will require the support and assistance of their community.

Bradford, to me, is a city of the future: multi-faith, ethnically diverse, with roots in both English history and cultures around the world. It's a city that has embraced newcomers and is hungry for growth – as the success of the Bradford Literature Festival has shown. But it's also a city that must keep improving: in the services we rely on, the jobs young people can aspire to, the homes they dream of building their lives in.

There are Bradfords all over the world – cities beyond the metropolitan centres, where life is lived by people who value community and collaboration over division and distrust.

Politics should be about bringing people together, rather than driving them apart. Everyone deserves the opportunity to thrive – to live in peace with your family, your neighbours and your wider community. My aim, like many others around the world, is simple: to help build a future where everyone has the freedom to hope, to belong and to get on with their lives.

And I am genuinely optimistic about that future. The way things are now – where opportunists take advantage of division, instead of working to bring people together – can't go on. Those of us elected to serve have a responsibility to take that seriously. It's not about ego or power, but about doing right by the people who trusted us with their votes. That means staying focused, staying honest and not giving up – no matter how long it takes.

A long time ago I learnt that to be an effective leader, you must be authentic and sincere. People can tell when you're being real – honesty matters. When I look around at my colleagues in Westminster or watch Sky News reporting from America or India or China, I see too many people in positions of power who are acting inauthentically.

Real leadership isn't just for the workplace or politics – it shows up in everyday life as well. I try to bring the same principles to raising my kids as I do to my work. Every week, we set aside at least an hour to say exactly what we might want to get off our chests. Nothing is off limits. As a parent, it's on me to help make sense of things and create space for honesty. It doesn't matter if someone gets upset during the process – what matters is that no one feels guilty for problems not of their own making, that the right conversations take place and that we move forward. That is how we grow – as people, as families, as society – one honest exchange at a time.

There's a very fine line between owning your power as a leader and becoming blasé about it – between recognising what leadership can achieve and simply enjoying being in charge. I have an ego and I need validation; I'm not super-human. The trouble begins when ego starts to drive your decisions. Thankfully, I have enough brave people around me who will call me out if they witness me becoming a little too pleased with myself and my position – whether that's my kids, my siblings or a fellow politician.

The great leaders and campaigners I've admired throughout

my life – particularly those from Black communities – have held their strength with grace and congruence. Do Black leaders need to work harder than white leaders to be heard? Without a doubt. Does that make successful Black leaders more effective than white leaders? Good question!

All this brings me back to faith. Mine is a constant guide – a framework for how I try to live my life. I've been lucky enough to see many of my dreams come true, and it would be easy to convince myself that I made it all happen on my own. But that is just ego – or what we call *nafs*.

If your higher purpose is to serve God, then personal ambition comes second to the good you want to do. I see my life as a gift and I'm obliged to use it in the service of others. You don't need to be Muslim to live by the right values – you may have your own faith, or no faith at all. But for me, Islam gives me three guiding principles that keep me on the straight and narrow: tawakkul (trusting in God's plan), nafs (ego) and *doha* (prayer). And perhaps most important of all: the humility to understand you are the conduit in the temporary world to deliver the best you can achieve.

Community is one of the foundational pillars of human life. My mum and I learnt the hard way that your community can be tough on you; it can turn its back on you when it perceives you've stepped out of line. Although Mum can be infuriating at times, she has inspired me through her own relationship with her community. Even when her people let go of her, she didn't let go of them and it was her knowledge of the importance of those around her which gave her the strength to keep going, to be resilient.

One of the many reasons I'm grateful to you for reading this far is that the process of writing this book has revealed to me just how much strength I have gathered from my community.

Like Mum, I've suffered at the hands of social media trolls and entrenched baradari conspiracists who wanted to do me harm. As recently as 2022, despite all the progress I've made in building the foundations of a better future for my constituents in Bradford West, I was the victim of a concerted baradari attempt to oust me as the Labour candidate for the next election.

Thankfully, my allies defended me and ultimately their campaign was defeated, but it was yet another painful reminder that, for reasons which are nothing at all to do with my work on behalf of my constituents and on behalf of Muslims worldwide, there will always be a small group of male clan members who want me to lose.

There's a well-known tale in Pakistan about the frog who never escapes his pond and never discovers the joys of the river and the surrounding countryside. These baradari men are like little pond frogs: too scared to move beyond their tiny, enclosed conspiracy groups, and too limited in their outlook to see anything beyond their blind clan allegiances. If they moved out of these surroundings, ill-equipped as they are, they would quickly come face to face with their irrelevance in the wider world; they simply don't have what it takes to be in charge.

It astonishes me that after almost a decade of service, where I have worked my heart out to boost opportunities for the people of Bradford, they would still rather throw that all away simply out of misogynistic malice.

But ultimately, it's their tragedy – a tragedy of petty, mean spite.

I get it: I'm a brown, female, feminist Member of Parliament. I don't shy away from the spotlight and I won't back down in the face of intimidation. So I understand that there will always be people who, for their own twisted reasons, want to have a go at me, undermine my position and watch me suffer. But I don't lose much sleep over it – because every day, I'm buoyed by the strength and solidarity of the community that stands with me.

I cannot eradicate Islamophobia or antisemitism. Nor can I bring peace to the Middle East. But that isn't what is being asked of me. In my religion, Allah asks us to live a life of purpose, to be the best that we can be.

Of course, the fight for justice is tough and the struggle will be long, as we face the many challenges ahead in a divisive world. But we all need to ask ourselves some essential questions if we are to live fulfilling and purposeful lives.

How do we help people feel like they truly belong? How do we ensure unity and humanity triumph over division and hatred?

How do we keep a light burning in the dark days?

The answers are simple: compassion, empathy and courage.

As a Muslim none of this is an option; it is a requirement of my faith. And to be an effective MP for my community, I hold true to the principles of my faith.

It took me a while to immerse myself completely in my faith and give in to its wisdom and guidance, but when the time was right and I fully embraced Islam, I wasn't reproached for my slow pace but greeted with open arms. My religion has never let me down, even as I struggled to hold on to my sanity, my hope and my family.

We survived. But more than that, with God's grace we continue to thrive.

Epilogue

It's late September and I'm sitting in my house in Bradford putting the finishing touches to this book. This year, we had the hottest summer the world has ever recorded. And we had our fair share of the heat, too, the sun beating down on the yellow sandstone of Bradford's houses day after day. It's a British thing, obviously: always start a conversation with the weather.

These days, though, you can't even talk about the weather in isolation. We may have had some lovely days here, but elsewhere in the world there have been floods and fires and earthquakes. None of us lives in isolation any longer; we're more connected than we have ever been, through social media and endless news channels. But while we know much more about each other, I question whether it's brought us any closer.

Even as we close the distance between us, we face increasingly threatening calls for division, siren voices from all ends of the political spectrum – and across the world – urging conflict, confrontation and control.

I have served as a Labour MP for over a decade now. In 2023, around the time the idea for this book ignited, I realised that I wanted us all to be properly rooted at home again and so the boys went back in school in Bradford while their elder

EPILOGUE

sister began university. Bradford is where my family lives, it's the place that truly defines me.

Bradford is a city of half a million people, a city that was built on the labour of men and women in the mills of the nineteenth-century industrial revolution. I was born here in 1973 and have lived here my whole life, except for when I was away in Pakistan, and when we were moving between Bradford, Leeds and Sheffield. It's a very special place for me, like your hometown may be for you. Maybe like yours, it's a multicultural city – Bradford has almost 30 per cent Asian residents alongside a majority white population. It's a city that has struggled during years of austerity and industrial decline, a place that still has unacceptable pockets of poverty.

There's something else about Bradford, though. To me, it represents the future, containing the seeds of how we might all live if we could shift the divisive paradigms that seem to have engulfed us over the last twenty years or so. I feel as though Bradford, like other cities around the world that are situated a long way away from their national capitals, stands for how we would all want to live.

I regularly drive past the bus stop near Legrams Lane where my mum burst into tears because she was lost and alone with three young children in tow. I can still see the look of confusion and fear on her face, tears streaming down her cheeks, while Foz and Imy and I watched on in horror – what was happening to our mum? But then I'll drive on, maybe stop by at the drive-in chai counter to pick up a ginger tea and a samosa, or maybe I'll keep on going to the carpet shop to choose a new rug for one of the kids' bedrooms or head to the town hall for a meeting with the chief executive of the council. I am completely immersed in my community, full to the brim with it.

This sense of community isn't a parochial, small-town thing. It's the complete opposite. The fact that I had the honour of making the Global Muslim 500 List in 2022 is because the community feeling I have for Bradford has broadened to embrace a global community. This, I am convinced, is the route for us all to improve the world in which we live: to see the entire planet as an extension of the community from which we emerged. It's true that we're living in turbulent times, with too many divisive figures encouraging us to square up to one another rather than find connection. This isn't how any of us, at heart, want to live. We want to exist in safety as members of a community, and the streets where I buy my ginger tea and samosas are just as much part of my community as any other street in any other city in the world.

Our society is made up of people of all faiths and beliefs and cultures, and we're bound together by our desire to live alongside each other in harmony. Our family can accommodate all kinds of rifts and arguments, but the family bond, if it is real, will always overcome division.

And within our community, our faith is what keeps each one of us steady, whether we're Muslim, Jewish, Christian or humanist – it's more powerful than anything, more powerful than money, more powerful than ambition. I'm proud of my career and my job is a huge part of what defines me. I've put my life's energy into my work. But equally, I have no attachment to it. That's where the power comes in, that's what faith teaches you: nothing belongs to you.

EPILOGUE

I don't underestimate the challenges we all face, both as politicians and as voters, to repair the damage to our society. My own belief is that it could take us ten or fifteen years to recover that sense of community, to rid our politics of division and to replace it with the simple fundamental principles of equality, fairness and justice. My own community of Bradford has given me the inner strength and inspiration to build a global vision of a future where we nurture and nourish rather than compete and control.

And I'm not the only one.

Make no mistake: this movement is growing all over the world.

In Islam, whenever anyone dies, we say: to God we belong and to God we return. By that definition, everything on this earth – our children included – is a gift from God. When we accept that, we can let go of our attachment to worldly things. We have to understand that everything we have could be gone tomorrow.

In my own life, I have learnt this in a very immediate way. Time and again, and from a very young age, I lost my security, my sense of home. I slept in crack houses when I was homeless, attempted suicide and suffered death threats. Yet I've also stood up in the most famous political arena in the world and given speeches; I've borne three fantastic children who have never felt displaced or lacked a place to call home.

My faith has taught me that I'm not in control of my life: God is. This is not to say we can't strive for success or follow our ambition – that's our human nature. Because, if God has gifted me with anything, it's that I must honour His faith

EPILOGUE

in my abilities and use that ability to do good. My faith has taught me that God expects me to try to be the best that I can be. My 'gift', if you like, is the ability to campaign on behalf of others, and I have devoted my entire career to that end. But I also know that everything can be taken away from me at any moment, and if that is God's will, then so be it. I know for an absolute fact that if I had to go back to packing faulty nappies, then I wouldn't have any issue whatsoever. It is what it is.

She's funny, my mum. She's been through more trauma than most people; that much is obvious by now. She hid her pain and torment from her three children for years, while she rocked and cried herself to sleep in front of the single-bar electric fire, taking absolutely any job she could find in order to keep us clothed and fed. Now she has her own lovely apartment in my brother's house, and she can join me at a posh event in Bradford where we're the guests of honour. Neither scenario means more than the other, and I know she understands that as well as I do because of faith. Faith, when you look at it this way, provides you with enough resilience to face the challenges life throws your way, as I hope I have demonstrated within the pages of this book. And it is resilience which lies at the heart of the human condition.

Mum learnt the hard way that in a patriarchal culture, the honour is always held by the men while the shame is carried by women. She was held to blame for the breakup of our family when my dad ran off with the neighbour's daughter. She was held to blame when the man who said he'd help her in her ambition to buy a family home turned out to be a

EPILOGUE

violent rapist and drug dealer. I wasn't allowed to possess any sense of honour as a young girl, because I came from a family that had lost its father.

Between us, though, we've regained our place in the community. We've never – either of us – turned away from an opportunity to heal a rift rather than underline it. Even in the depths of our despair and poverty when, from the age of six, I dragged my belongings from place to place in a black bin liner, Mum would embrace any chance to show respect to a member of the wider family or community. As I've said, she is always the first with a gift for the happy couple on their wedding day, always the first with a baby blanket for a new arrival, and always first in line to offer respects to the family who have just lost a loved one. There's no holding Mum back from what she views as her community duty.

There are times when Mum is over at my house, sitting by the fire because she feels the cold, maybe drying her hair after a shower. She's not crying – she rarely cries these days – but as she gently towels her hair she can appear lost in thought. There is no doubt that those fourteen years in prison took their toll, leaving a hollow space inside her, despite the loving company of her family – not to mention the preceding years of abandonment and abuse.

Mum is finally living the life she always wanted. And she never wanted much, simply a home, a family, a future. Now she has five grandchildren to watch over. She enjoys their company, smiling to herself as they giggle over a joke. I know she's thinking what I'm thinking: we're both so desperately happy that these children can live normal, peaceful lives just like other kids. We don't talk about what happened to her, and we probably never will. We both know what we went through to get to this point.

And yet, she can still drive me absolutely mad. I might be trying to talk to my kids about equality between the sexes and she'll pipe up with a crazy theory or two. The one I've had to stop her from ever repeating is where she compares a woman to a cat. In the same way you have to train a cat to stop jumping onto surfaces where it doesn't belong, a *woman* needs similar discipline. According to Mum, women have restless natures and need men to rein them in – tame their wild ways, so to speak. A cat needs boundaries, and so do women. She'll make this comparison as though it's an obvious fact. 'What the hell, Mum?' I say to her whenever she graces us with her arcane wisdom. But to her credit, with a little unpacking and a little reflection, she always gets there in the end and can even laugh at herself.

That's just part of being human, though, isn't it? Your family and your community are so dear to you, and yet each of us is able to annoy the hell out of one another.

I can drive my sister, Foz, crazy when I take calls in the middle of a conversation. I get on my mum's nerves if I interrupt one of her Pakistani soap operas. My daughter, Leyana, set me a challenge recently by deciding to wear the hijab, which I never have. She's just as forthright a feminist as me, maybe even more so, and yet her decision is based on her own understanding of her faith and her own conception of the society around her. I'm proud of her boldness, proud of her ability to forge her own path and challenge mine when she thinks I've gone astray.

As I mentioned earlier my and my siblings' childhoods

EPILOGUE

affected each of us in different ways. They both live respectful, observant lives. The concept of respect is embedded in our very bones and because our mother was dishonoured, the efforts we went to reclaim our izzat – while certainly tough at times and more than a little heart-breaking – felt very natural to us. Very simply, it was our destiny to fight for Mum. Watching her public humiliation made me vow that my children would never endure the same shame. While I am regularly featured in the press, it's for my work, and for being publicly validated. My mother was tried by a jury, found guilty by the people, and yet her daughter is being cheered by those who voted for her. I feel I have upheld the honour of my family.

There is no question: I am honoured that you have chosen to read my book. I hope I have repaid your curiosity by giving it to you straight; by telling you how I have felt about what many would undoubtedly term an eventful life, but which to me seems to have a logic all of its own. If I hadn't lived through my experiences – the pain, the happiness, the tears and the joy – I wouldn't be able, now in my mid-fifties, to feel my overwhelming sense of anticipation for the future. The events of my life have all contributed in one way or another to making me the person I am today. They have forged within me a determination to keep going, to keep striving on behalf of the community – at home and around the world.

What comes next? I don't know and it's not my place to plan. All I know is that I am on a path that can lead to a better world, and I see plenty of others walking beside me. I have skills, determination and resilience to offer, but I'm not foolish enough to think that I know any better than anyone

EPILOGUE

else. If the lessons of my life can be of use to others, then in all humility I offer them. I treasure our shared sense of a future and I'm ready to help build it.

There is going to be a better future which we will all celebrate, a future where equality, fairness and justice belong to all, not just the few. As we work towards it, I hope I'll meet some of you along the way.

Please keep me in your prayers.

Acknowledgements

Writing this book has stirred a depth of emotions, from tears of pain rooted in the past to tears of joy as I look upon the blessings that have shaped me and brought me to where I stand today.

Through those shared struggles which have marked this journey, I want to first acknowledge my mother, Zoora, my brother, Imy, and my sister, Foz, for their unwavering love and the role they have played in my life.

I also acknowledge with deepest gratitude my children, Leyana, Aydan and Raese, who are both my strength and my inspiration for all that lies ahead.

To my immediate family; the father of my children, Lee; my sister-in-law; my sister Fozia's husband, Pav; and my niece and nephew, Inaya and Shavez; thank you for being my foundation.

Thank you to my Mamu Iqbal for his support.

To my friends who carried me through the tears of reliving past horrors and supported me unfailingly along the way: Jude, Soby, Sam, Nazia, Yazmin, Komal, Syima, Salima, Caryl, Carol and Bhaji Shamim.

To the family members who reached out and tried to help during my most difficult times, in particular my late uncle,

ACKNOWLEDGEMENTS

Khadim, who I miss dearly, Uncle Pav and cousins, including Shamim. Thanks also to the Samaritans, whose compassion and presence reminded me that no one is ever truly alone.

To my mentors past and present, in particular Dr Eden Charles, Ali Jan Haider and Ziauddin Sardar, for their wisdom and guidance.

To my Parliamentary staff team past and present, with particular gratitude to my senior leadership team: Muhbeen Hussain, Ibrar Hussain and Asma Shabbir.

To Mudassar Ahmed, along with Prof Saeed Khan and the wider Concordia alumni family, locally, nationally and globally, for opening doors to a network of exceptional leaders and thinkers who have enriched my journey through continuous learning, profound one-to-one exchanges of knowledge and experience, and opportunities without limit. Your counsel, encouragement and solidarity have been deeply valued.

To my brothers in faith and in humanity, Shaykh Dr Hisham Hellyer, Shaykh Sharif Banna MBE, Shaykh Abdalhaqq Bewley, Mufti Hassan Raza and Bishop Toby Howarth, who picked up their phones at unearthly hours when I needed support.

To my political allies locally, regionally and nationally, who stood beside me during the toughest moments – especially when I was fighting against misogynistic and vitriolic political campaigns in Bradford West – especially my Labour family and election agents.

To the Bradford business community, whose leadership in both politics and business has always embodied a vision of hope for Bradford and beyond, refusing to shrink into small

ACKNOWLEDGEMENTS

thinking or clan politics. The friendships and encouragement have been invaluable both to me personally and to the broader vision we share for our city.

To my team at Weidenfeld & Nicolson, especially Jenny Lord for her unwavering guidance and support. Many thanks to Alexandra Pringle for introducing me to my wonderful agent, Victoria Hobbs, who has beautifully explained to me exactly how publishing works. Huge thanks to both Simon Petheridge and Arzu Tahsin for persevering with my many digressions and sticking with me until I reached my destination.

Above all, my deepest gratitude is to the people of Bradford West, for your faith, love and unwavering support. You have honoured me with the privilege of being your voice in Parliament. At times, I may have been the unluckiest of candidates, facing repeated toxic campaigns, but I have also been the luckiest, because you saw through it all and chose to stand by me, even in the hardest of moments.

The list is endless. Were I to continue, these acknowledgements would themselves become a book. So I also extend my heartfelt thanks to those I have not named here, for the support, guidance and prayers that have sustained me throughout this journey. Any success in these pages is by God's grace; the errors are mine alone.

RAISING READERS
Books Build Bright Futures

Dear Reader,

We'd love your attention for one more page to tell you about the crisis in children's reading, and what we can all do.

Studies have shown that reading for fun is the **single biggest predictor of a child's future life chances** – more than family circumstance, parents' educational background or income. It improves academic results, mental health, wealth, communication skills, ambition and happiness.[1]

The number of children reading for fun is in rapid decline. Young people have a lot of competition for their time. In 2024, 1 in 10 children and young people in the UK aged 5 to 18 did not own a single book at home.[2]

Hachette works extensively with schools, libraries and literacy charities, but here are some ways we can all raise more readers:

- Reading to children for just 10 minutes a day makes a difference
- Don't give up if children aren't regular readers – there will be books for them!
- Visit bookshops and libraries to get recommendations
- Encourage them to listen to audiobooks
- Support school libraries
- Give books as gifts

There's a lot more information about how to encourage children to read on our website: **www.RaisingReaders.co.uk**

Thank you for reading.

---

[1] OECD, '21st-Century Readers: Developing Literacy Skills in a Digital World', 2021, https://www.oecd.org/en/publications/21st-century-readers_a83d84cb-en.html

[2] National Literacy Trust, 'Book Ownership in 2024', November 2024, https://literacytrust.org.uk/research-services/research-reports/book-ownership-in-2024